Enhancing Articulation and Transfer

Carolyn Prager, *Editor*

NEW DIRECTIONS FOR COMMUNITY COLLEGES
ARTHUR M. COHEN, *Editor-in-Chief*
FLORENCE B. BRAWER, *Associate Editor*

Number 61, Spring 1988

Paperback sourcebooks in
The Jossey-Bass Higher Education Series

Jossey-Bass Inc., Publishers
San Francisco • London

Carolyn Prager (ed.).
Enhancing Articulation and Transfer.
New Directions for Community Colleges, no. 61.
Volume XVI, number 1.
San Francisco: Jossey-Bass, 1988.

New Directions for Community Colleges
Arthur M. Cohen, *Editor-in-Chief;* Florence B. Brawer, *Associate Editor*

New Directions for Community Colleges is published quarterly by Jossey-Bass Inc., Publishers (publication number USPS 121-710), in association with the ERIC Clearinghouse for Junior Colleges. *New Directions* is numbered sequentially—please order extra copies by sequential number. The volume and issue numbers above are included for the convenience of libraries. Second-class postage paid at San Francisco, California, and at additional mailing offices. POSTMASTER: Send address changes to Jossey-Bass, Inc., Publishers, 350 Sansome Street, San Francisco, California 94104.

The material in this publication was prepared pursuant to a contract with the Office of Educational Research and Improvement, U.S. Department of Education. Contractors undertaking such projects under government sponsorship are encouraged to express freely their judgment in professional and technical matters. Prior to publication, the manuscript was submitted to the Center for the Study of Community Colleges for critical review and determination of professional competence. This publication has met such standards. Points of view or opinions, however, do not necessarily represent the official view or opinions of the Center for the Study of Community Colleges or the Office of Educational Research and Improvement.

Editorial correspondence should be sent to the Editor-in-Chief, Arthur M. Cohen, at the ERIC Clearinghouse for Junior Colleges, University of California, Los Angeles, California 90024.

Library of Congress Catalog Card Number LC 85-644753

International Standard Serial Number ISSN 0194-3081

International Standard Book Number ISBN 1-55542-912-2

Cover art by WILLI BAUM

Manufactured in the United States of America

Ordering Information

The paperback sourcebooks listed below are published quarterly and can be ordered either by subscription or single copy.

Subscriptions cost $52.00 per year for institutions, agencies, and libraries. Individuals can subscribe at the special rate of $39.00 per year *if payment is by personal check.* (Note that the full rate of $52.00 applies if payment is by institutional check, even if the subscription is designated for an individual.) Standing orders are accepted.

Single copies are available at $12.95 when payment accompanies order. (California, New Jersey, New York, and Washington, D.C., residents please include appropriate sales tax.) For billed orders, cost per copy is $12.95 plus postage and handling.

Substantial discounts are offered to organizations and individuals wishing to purchase bulk quantities of Jossey-Bass sourcebooks. Please inquire.

Please note that these prices are for the calendar year 1988 and are subject to change without notice. Also, some titles may be out of print and therefore not available for sale.

To ensure correct and prompt delivery, all orders must give either the *name of an individual* or an *official purchase order number.* Please submit your order as follows:

Subscriptions: specify series and year subscription is to begin.
Single Copies: specify sourcebook code (such as, CC1) and first two words of title.

Mail orders for United States and Possessions, Australia, New Zealand, Canada, Latin America, and Japan to:
Jossey-Bass Inc., Publishers
350 Sansome Street
San Francisco, California 94104

Mail orders for all other parts of the world to:
Jossey-Bass Limited
28 Banner Street
London EC1Y 8QE

New Directions for Community Colleges Series
Arthur M. Cohen, *Editor-in-Chief*
Florence B. Brawer, *Associate Editor*

CC1 *Toward a Professional Faculty,* Arthur M. Cohen
CC2 *Meeting the Financial Crisis,* John Lombardi
CC3 *Understanding Diverse Students,* Dorothy M. Knoell

CC4 *Updating Occupational Education,* Norman C. Harris
CC5 *Implementing Innovative Instruction,* Roger H. Garrison
CC6 *Coordinating State Systems,* Edmund J. Gleazer, Jr., Roger Yarrington
CC7 *From Class to Mass Learning,* William M. Birenbaum
CC8 *Humanizing Student Services,* Clyde E. Blocker
CC9 *Using Instructional Technology,* George H. Voegel
CC10 *Reforming College Governance,* Richard C. Richardson, Jr.
CC11 *Adjusting to Collective Bargaining,* Richard J. Ernst
CC12 *Merging the Humanities,* Leslie Koltai
CC13 *Changing Managerial Perspectives,* Barry Heermann
CC14 *Reaching Out Through Community Service,* Hope M. Holcomb
CC15 *Enhancing Trustee Effectiveness,* Victoria Dziuba, William Meardy
CC16 *Easing the Transition from Schooling to Work,* Harry F. Silberman, Mark B. Ginsburg
CC17 *Changing Instructional Strategies,* James O. Hammons
CC18 *Assessing Student Academic and Social Progress,* Leonard L. Baird
CC19 *Developing Staff Potential,* Terry O'Banion
CC20 *Improving Relations with the Public,* Louis W. Bender, Benjamin R. Wygal
CC21 *Implementing Community-Based Education,* Ervin L. Harlacher, James F. Gollatscheck
CC22 *Coping with Reduced Resources,* Richard L. Alfred
CC23 *Balancing State and Local Control,* Searle F. Charles
CC24 *Responding to New Missions,* Myron A. Marty
CC25 *Shaping the Curriculum,* Arthur M. Cohen
CC26 *Advancing International Education,* Maxwell C. King, Robert L. Breuder
CC27 *Serving New Populations,* Patricia Ann Walsh
CC28 *Managing in a New Era,* Robert E. Lahti
CC29 *Serving Lifelong Learners,* Barry Heermann, Cheryl Coppeck Enders, Elizabeth Wine
CC30 *Using Part-Time Faculty Effectively,* Michael H. Parsons
CC31 *Teaching the Sciences,* Florence B. Brawer
CC32 *Questioning the Community College Role,* George B. Vaughan
CC33 *Occupational Education Today,* Kathleen F. Arns
CC34 *Women in Community Colleges,* Judith S. Eaton
CC35 *Improving Decision Making,* Mantha Mehallis
CC36 *Marketing the Program,* William A. Keim, Marybelle C. Keim
CC37 *Organization Development: Change Strategies,* James Hammons
CC38 *Institutional Impacts on Campus, Community, and Business Constituencies,* Richard L. Alfred
CC39 *Improving Articulation and Transfer Relationships,* Frederick C. Kintzer
CC40 *General Education in Two-Year Colleges,* B. Lamar Johnson
CC41 *Evaluating Faculty and Staff,* Al Smith
CC42 *Advancing the Liberal Arts,* Stanley F. Turesky
CC43 *Counseling: A Crucial Function for the 1980s,* Alice S. Thurston, William A. Robbins
CC44 *Strategic Management in the Community College,* Gunder A. Myran
CC45 *Designing Programs for Community Groups,* S. V. Martorana, William E. Piland
CC46 *Emerging Roles for Community College Leaders,* Richard L. Alfred, Paul A. Elsner, R. Jan LeCroy, Nancy Armes
CC47 *Microcomputer Applications in Administration and Instruction,* Donald A. Dellow, Lawrence H. Poole

CC48 *Customized Job Training for Business and Industry,* Robert J. Kopecek, Robert G. Clarke
CC49 *Ensuring Effective Governance,* William L. Deegan, James F. Gollattscheck
CC50 *Strengthening Financial Management,* Dale F. Campbell
CC51 *Active Trusteeship for a Changing Era,* Gary Frank Petty
CC52 *Maintaining Institutional Integrity,* Donald E. Puyear, George B. Vaughan
CC53 *Controversies and Decision Making in Difficult Economic Times,* Billie Wright Dziech
CC54 *The Community College and Its Critics,* L. Stephen Zwerling
CC55 *Advances in Instructional Technology,* George H. Voegel
CC56 *Applying Institutional Research,* John Losak
CC57 *Teaching the Developmental Education Student,* Kenneth M. Ahrendt
CC58 *Developing Occupational Programs,* Charles R. Doty
CC59 *Issues in Student Assessment,* Dorothy Bray, Marcia J. Belcher
CC60 *Marketing Strategies for Changing Times,* Wellford W. Wilms, Richard W. Moore

Contents

Editor's Notes

Most comprehensive community college mission statements list the transfer function as the first of the institution's missions. Nevertheless, there is considerable evidence that transfer has declined during the period in which most of those reading this page have been associated with community colleges. Mission schizophrenia is apparent at every level of community college life. The public continues to perceive transfer education as the foremost purpose of the community college (Knoell, 1982). The majority of students have the baccalaureate degree as their goal when they enter the community college (Cohen, Brawer, and Bensimon, 1985). However, few faculty—only 19 percent according to a recent study—believe that the primary mission of the community college should be preparation for transfer (Cohen, Brawer, and Bensimon, 1985). Indeed, in their attempts to carve out a unique niche for public two-year colleges in higher education, some community college leaders prominent at the national level have eschewed the transfer role in favor of such functions as community services and lifelong learning (Gleazer, 1980; Gollattscheck and others, 1976) or vocational training (Parnell, 1985).

For a variety of reasons, it is no longer tenable to counter the criticism that transfer has been devalued over the past two decades or more (Zwerling, 1986) with the claim that community colleges have emphasized other and more distinctive functions instead. For one, community colleges continue to serve as the major gateway to higher education for minorities, a phenomenon that converts transfer from a purely educational process into a social imperative (Olivas, 1979; Avila and others, 1983). For another, community colleges cannot afford to lose potential liberal arts and science transfer students to other market forces in a period of declining enrollment pools. Such losses are likely to happen unless the public two-year college demonstrates that it can provide freshman and sophomore education as good as, if not superior to, that provided by competing senior institutions. For still another, publicly mandated accountability measures, such as Florida's College-Level Academic Skills Test or New Jersey's projected value-added test for fourth-semester students, will test the claim that community colleges provide a different but qualitatively equal form of collegiate education. Perhaps the most compelling reason is that if the community college is to maintain an organic rather than a merely regulated connection to higher education, it must reassert its collegiate identity within a continuum that leads potentially to the baccalaureate and beyond.

The reaffirmation of a collegiate identity for the community college within the larger higher education framework defines articulation in its broadest sense (Deegan and Tillery, 1985). However, certain articulation variables have changed a great deal since the early years of the community college movement. Students who transfer not only move from one academic level to another but also from one distinctively different institutional culture to another, usually to one that they describe as less nurturing than that of the community college (Richardson and Bender, 1986). Therefore, to improve transfer viability, transfer education must go beyond the search for academic parallelism in freshman and sophomore studies at the two- and four-year levels by including intellectual, social, and cultural preparation for the baccalaureate environment.

In addition to reformulating transfer education so that it includes education about transfer, transfer education needs to be refocused to include education for all those who seek to transfer, regardless of academic track. Indeed, the fact that the transfer rate of occupational-technical students now equals or exceeds that of liberal arts and science students calls into question the validity of distinguishing between these two groups in terms of transfer and nontransfer tracks. It also calls into question the adequacy of career program preparation for baccalaureate degree study and of baccalaureate degree educational options for career students, as Carolyn Prager notes in Chapter Nine. Finally, the community college drift away from senior college–determined curriculum content, pacing, and standards has exacerbated the difficulties of restoring academically valid ties between two- and four-year programs of undergraduate instruction. Restoration of these ties may require community college faculty to acknowledge that their autonomy to decide curriculum is as limited as that of freshman and sophomore instructors in any four-year undergraduate department or program.

The perceived deterioration of the transfer function has prompted intervention by extramural bodies, including state agencies and legislatures, interstate commissions, and private foundations. Florida has legislated and continues to legislate a multifaceted secondary-postsecondary articulated system that ranges from common course numbering to resource sharing to systemwide data gathering, which Robert S. Palinchak discusses in Chapter Two. California appropriated $3.373 million dollars in 1985 for the first year of a three-year project that features highly visible community college campus transfer centers along with Project ASSIST, a computerized course and program information system incorporating course-equivalency data and articulation information (Dyste and Miner, 1986). The Fund for the Improvement of Post-Secondary Education (FIPSE) has funded the Western Interstate Commission for Higher Education (WICHE) regional project, which has as its major focus the development of computerized student information systems that would provide students and their advisers in three states with current information about course transfers.

The Ford Foundation, through the Urban Community College Transfer Opportunities Program (UCCTOP), has funded twenty-four projects aimed at improving minority transfer through special support services, testing, curriculum development, and articulation negotiation (Cohen, Brawer, and Bensimon, 1985). The Andrew W. Mellon Foundation has sponsored similar programs at twelve baccalaureate degree-granting institutions to increase the movement of graduates, especially minorities, from neighboring community colleges into their programs.

In reviewing the reports and studies that have emanated from these extramurally conceived and funded projects, one is struck by the frequency with which their authors conclude that the single most promising strategy for reducing transfer barriers is intermural faculty exchange and communication. Most of the chapters in this volume reflect that finding, whether their authors write from the perspective of the two-year college, the four-year college or university, a university system, or a state coordinating agency. By contrast, Richard D. McCrary describes in Chapter Eight an alternative student services approach to articulation that relies most prominently on print information.

Many chapters in this volume reflect efforts to improve transfer by creating vehicles and channels for interinstitutional faculty contact. In Chapter Three, Dympna Bowles places such efforts in the context of universitywide discussions about liberal arts and science course transferability. In Chapter Four, Renee Berger and Aida M. Ortiz Ruiz locate them in the context of increasing minority student transfer opportunities at an urban institution. In certain areas, external accreditation guidelines govern the entire four-year program sequence. In Chapter Five, Gary Thomas shows how such guidelines affect the articulation of engineering technology, and in Chapter Six, Mary Robertson-Smith discusses their effect on efforts to articulate business curricula. In Chapter Seven, Elizabeth C. King relates transfer improvement to attempts to determine the competence bases for allied health transfer agreements, and in Chapter One, Kenneth B. Woodbury, Jr., describes the faculty exchanges that form the backdrop to the evolution of articulation into programs of dual admissions.

Taken together, these chapters anticipate a new direction to transfer and articulation activities that will be concerned as much if not more with academic as with procedural underpinnings. The groundwork for increasingly effective two- and four-year programmatic and institutional relationships has been laid through improvement in the mechanics of negotiation and coordination, delivery of transfer information to students, and encouragement of student transfer. As a result, the community colleges are ready to address underlying academic issues concerned with the quality of student preparation for a baccalaureate environment.

There is sufficient preliminary evidence to suggest that community college studies lack the rigor they now should have. For example, a survey of 444 randomly selected faculty teaching transferable courses at the twenty-four UCCTOP community colleges revealed that 45 percent of the faculty gave no essay exams and that essay tests counted for no more than 25 percent of a course grade for most of those who did (Cohen, Brawer, and Bensimon, 1985). Other studies suggest that fragmented learning processes and inadequate academic skills orientation in many community college courses undermine attempts to maintain university parallelism through recourse to comparable texts and curriculum objectives (Richardson and Bender, 1986).

These findings are significant because they confirm the concern about community college standards and pedagogy that is not always voiced in transfer and articulation discussions between faculty of two- and four-year colleges. While all sectors of higher education and their governing bodies must share responsibility for the historic deterioration of academic ties between associate and baccalaureate degree-granting institutions, only the community colleges can accept responsibility for strengthening the quality of students' preparation for academic transfer. The authors of the chapters in this volume describe some of the current policies and practices of transfer and articulation that mark the return of community colleges to the academy and lay the groundwork for continuity in the discussion about the academic quality of transfer preparation. We have every expectation that this discussion will continue.

Carolyn Prager
Editor

References

Avila, J. G., Baller, M. J., Brown, S. E., and Vera, R. T. *Petition to Increase Minority Transfer from Community Colleges to State Four-Year Schools.* San Francisco: Mexican American Legal Defense and Educational Fund, Inc., 1983. 37 pp. (ED 237 134)

Cohen, A. M., Brawer, F. B., and Bensimon, E. M. *Transfer Education in American Community Colleges.* Los Angeles: Center for the Study of Community Colleges, 1985. 313 pp. (ED 255 250)

Deegan, W. L., and Tillery, D. "The Process of Renewal: An Agenda for Action." In W. L. Deegan, D. Tillery, and Associates, *Renewing the American Community College: Priorities and Strategies for Effective Leadership.* San Francisco: Jossey-Bass, 1985.

Dyste, R., and Miner, J. *Status Report on Transfer Center Pilot Program.* Sacramento: Office of the Chancellor, California Community Colleges, 1986. 24 pp. (ED 275 388)

Gleazer, E. J., Jr. *The Community College: Values, Vision, and Vitality.* Washington, D.C.: American Association of Community and Junior Colleges, 1980.

Gollattscheck, J. P., Harlacher, E. L., Roberts, E., and Wygal, B. R. *College Leadership for Community Renewal: Beyond Community-Based Education.* San Francisco: Jossey-Bass, 1976.

Knoell, D. "The Transfer Function—One of Many." In F. C. Kintzer (ed.), *Improving Articulation and Transfer Relationships.* New Directions for Community Colleges, no. 39. San Francisco: Jossey-Bass, 1982.

Olivas, M. A., with N. Alimba. *The Dilemma of Access: Minorities in Two-Year Colleges.* Washington, D.C.: Howard University Press, 1979.

Parnell, D. *The Neglected Majority.* Washington, D.C.: Community College Press, 1985.

Richardson, R. C., Jr., and Bender, L. W. *Helping Minorities Achieve Degrees: The Urban Connection. A Report to the Ford Foundation.* Tempe: Arizona State University, 1986. 228 pp. (ED 277 436)

Zwerling, L. S. (ed.). *The Community College and Its Critics.* New Directions for Community Colleges, no. 54. San Francisco: Jossey-Bass, 1986.

Carolyn Prager is former vice-president of academic affairs at Hudson County Community College, Jersey City, New Jersey, and former director of community colleges for the state of New Jersey.

Pennsylvania's pluralistic and decentralized system of public and private colleges has spawned creative approaches to lower- and upper-division articulation, including dual admissions.

Articulation and Dual Admissions

Kenneth B. Woodbury, Jr.

Since the inception of community colleges, four-year colleges and universities—transfer institutions—have accepted the graduates of two-year colleges and the courses that these students have completed at the two-year level. Indeed, the early development of the community college was premised on the concept of university parallelism in transfer curricula. Transfer has never been a simple issue of kind but rather a more complex issue of degree. How many credits can be counted toward the baccalaureate, and will they fulfill the distribution requirements of the transfer college? How many courses can be accepted toward the major? Are the general education courses compatible? Is the associate degree one half of the baccalaureate, or must additional course work be taken? Must courses required of freshmen or sophomores at the transfer college, such as physical education or Western culture, be completed by transfer students as juniors or seniors? What happens when transfer students change programs? Why are different credit hours calculated for similar courses?

A relatively recent approach in Pennsylvania has been to focus on transfer as a concept. This approach involves scrapping the numbers game and concentrating instead on the principles of transfer articulation. Establishment of such principles is a precondition for discussion between the community college and the transfer college. This approach has two

C. Prager (ed.). *Enhancing Articulation and Transfer.*
New Directions for Community Colleges, no. 61. San Francisco: Jossey-Bass, Spring 1988.

basic principles: first, to protect the integrity of the associate degree; second, to ensure that the community college transfer student receives equitable treatment from the transfer college.

Degree Integrity

The first principle is to assert that the associate degree represents the first half of a baccalaureate degree. It does not matter that the transfer colleges vary in total degree credits required or that associate degree credit hours vary by institution. Sixty associate degree credits should represent one half of a 120-credit-hour baccalaureate degree, just as 64 associate degree credits should equal one half of a 128-credit baccalaureate degree program. The transfer student should receive full and unequivocal junior class standing without having to complete additional course work normally taken at the lower-division level.

Several assumptions underlie the principles of degree integrity. The first is that the transfer student is seeking upper-division status in the same program completed for the associate degree. The second is that the associate degree that is earned has internal validity in order to be worthy of external acceptance. The associate degree has to stand on its own merits and represent more than a collection of courses with no rhyme or reason for their selection. The third assumption is that a minimum of sixty "clean" semester credits must be earned. That is, sixty credits must represent collegiate-level work reflecting courses normally found at the lower level in four-year colleges and universities. Thus, remedial, developmental, and literacy courses, advanced specialty courses usually reserved for juniors and seniors, career courses not normally included in an undergraduate baccalaureate program, and excess courses completed in a single discipline that total one half or more of the minimum credits for a declared major are excluded. The fourth assumption is that the transfer college can set a minimum exit standard for the award of an associate degree. The only restriction here is that the minimum grade point average acceptable for a community college graduate should not exceed the minimum acceptable to the transfer college for students transferring from the university's branch campus or from other collegiate institutions.

Equitable Treatment

The second principle is to ensure equitable treatment for the transfer student. This principle mandates that the transfer student should receive treatment identical to that afforded the transfer college's native junior student. Parity requires transfer students to receive consideration for campus housing on the same basis as native students of equal class standing. The same principle applies to such areas as financial aid, preregistration for junior classes, access to relevant student services, computation of academic honors, and dean's list status.

Program Articulation. Institutional transfer articulation does not preclude the possibility or even the desirability of program-by-program articulation. Some programs may require a higher earned grade point average than others do for admission. Program articulation agreements supplementing the institutional agreements should specify how transfer courses are to be treated. Transfer students want to know what courses most closely parallel the baccalaureate curriculum and how the community college courses will be counted. If a course completed at the lower-division level is specified as meeting requirements for the major rather than as a general elective, the transfer student's flexibility in the selection of courses resembles that enjoyed by other upper-division students.

Data Follow-Up. Articulation agreements should provide for follow-up services. Feedback on the transfer student's performance can be extremely valuable. The Buckley Amendment protecting the privacy of student information does not prevent the transfer college from sending student-identified transcripts to the sending college. Institutions wanting additional protection from student objections to the sharing of grade reports with the community college can either seek waivers from students or delete students' names from any grade reports that are sent. Without such information, the sending college can neither monitor the subsequent progress of its graduates nor compare their academic performance at the transfer institution with their associate degree records. With such information, departments and programs can determine whether their graduates experience any difficulties either overall or in specific courses. Such determinations are invaluable for program assessment, and they can guide community college faculty in curriculum and course improvement.

Diagnostic Testing. The articulation agreement should either specify that diagnostic testing may be done if required equally of native students (principle of parity) or ensure that transfer students earning a C or better in communication and computation courses will be waived from diagnostic testing (principle of degree integrity). On a related issue, the community college graduate who takes remedial-developmental courses should receive the same treatment as the native student who completes precollege work at the transfer college.

Transfer Worthiness over Time. Completion of the associate degree implies that the courses included are acceptable regardless of the date of completion. Time limits or other restrictions should be waived, with the possible exception of certain career courses in the nursing or allied health fields, where occupational currency and competence are a legitimate concern. However, expiration dates should not be applied to general education courses completed as part of an earned associate degree. That is, the community college should not be asked to accept that its courses lose transfer worthiness. It is unlikely that the transfer college would accept that its baccalaureate degree lose legitimacy over time.

Liaison. The articulation agreement should also require each institution to assign a staff member to serve as liaison. The liaison officer ensures maintenance of communication between the institution and acts as the campus watchdog and monitor.

Differences of Degree, Not Kind

Institutional agreements developed along the lines just described establish the twin principles of degree integrity and treatment parity. Once these issues have been settled on a broad basis, it becomes much easier to negotiate specific departmental or programmatic agreements. At the departmental level, issues of credit congruence, course descriptions, credit hours, general education requirements, core curricula, and treatment of required courses and elective credits are potentially divisive if protection of turf becomes paramount. The institutionwide agreement helps to establish the credentials and credibility of the community college as an equal partner in packaging a baccalaureate degree for the student. The community college guarantees the effectiveness and value of the lower-division work, and the transfer college guarantees the effectiveness and value of the upper-division work. Discussion and agreement about articulation should concern the proper fit between the two. The fit should be the focus of attention, not questions about the content of the other party's level.

One precondition for accepting transfer students is a recognition that the transfer college has delegated to the community college the right to designate the composition of the lower-division level, the freshman and sophomore years. The community college has met the same global accreditation standards as the four-year college, and the standards come from the same accrediting agency. It is not, then, proper to call its qualitative judgments into question. There are as many varieties of baccalaureate curricula within a given field as there are four-year colleges. Naturally, no community college two-year curriculum quite matches the lower-division work at any particular university. But, while differences are to be expected, they should be differences only of degree, not of kind. A four-year college that cannot recognize, tolerate, and accept these differences should not recruit community college transfer students.

Dual Admissions

It is only a short step, not a quantum leap, from articulation agreements developed according to the premises just outlined to dual admissions. Dual admissions has infinite benefits for the student, the two-year institution, and the transfer college. Essentially, dual admissions allows a high school senior to be admitted almost simultaneously to both a two-year and a four-year program, as a result of which the student's entire four-year sequence has been mapped before the student receives the high school diploma. Dual admissions allows for improved transfer counseling, since the entire lower-division curriculum can be tailored to the requirements of the designated transfer college. Such tailoring eliminates the questioning of transfer credits and offers the student certainty of treatment.

Bonding. Under dual admissions, the transfer college accepts an obligation to provide follow-up services to "its" student before the student matriculates as a junior. These activities are limited only by the creativity of the participating institutions. Among the standard fare is mailing the transfer college's student newspaper to the lower-division enrollee. This helps the community college student to identify and bond with the baccalaureate institution at the beginning of his or her college career. Periodic counseling by the transfer college, campus visits for special events, and mailings also strengthen the student's intention to complete the associate degree and to transfer.

Benefits. Dual admissions enables the transfer college to anticipate its junior transfer class. The process also provides it with an enhanced recruitment staff at high schools in the community college's area. Community college staff become extensions of the transfer college's admissions office, helping to promote both the community college and the baccalaureate institution.

Retention. The most obvious benefit that accrues to the community college under dual admissions is retention. Extending the student's goal from the associate degree to the bachelor's degree and offering a concrete path that enables the student to reach that goal helps to build student motivation. It also makes it easier to show the student why he or she should select particular courses and achieve academically.

Prestige by Association. Under dual admissions, the community college also gains the advantage of prestige by association. The two reasons why high school students say they are not interested in attending a community college—low tuition and open admissions—are, paradoxically, the major strengths of the community college. For many high school students, low tuition is synonymous with low quality, and open admissions is synonymous with social standardization.

The absence of elitism and barriers to entrance that is so attractive to the adult nontraditional student cuts at the self-esteem, personal pride, and peer acceptance so important to high school youth. Who wants to go to a college that anyone can attend regardless of academic achievement or family status? The community college acceptance letter is not apt to generate awe and excitement. However, acceptance at an expensive baccalaureate institution with selective admissions can be a source of pride and cause for excitement. The high school student may be reluctant to say that attendance at the community college precedes matriculation at the university, but the student can legitimately claim acceptance and intent to enroll at an institution that is more prestigious in his or her eyes.

Fiscal and Social Benefits. All students gain financially, and some students gain socially from the arrangement. For some, dual admissions may be the only way they can afford the more expensive transfer college. Some students may need the extra two years at home to mature and prepare to accept the responsibilities of an independent life.

Social Pluralism. Community colleges have successfully served as the Ellis Island of higher education. They have accepted the unprepared and underprepared learners who seek the job advancement and higher pay that comes from earning associate and baccalaureate degrees. Dual admissions allows a selective-admissions college to take a chance on a high school student that it would otherwise have rejected. The community college makes the extra financial and time commitment necessary to provide the extensive and intensive remedial-developmental support services and tutoring. Since transfer colleges can specify the junior entrance requirements, they can, without lowering their admissions standards, accept the marginal high school student who can help the transfer college to achieve a more pluralistic student body, and the transfer college knows that all academic deficiencies will have been remedied. As a result, the transfer college can concentrate on its major mission without having to dilute its efforts by providing remedial work, a mission that many find unfamiliar and that more traditional faculty find distasteful.

Dual Admissions and Interinstitutional Cooperation

Dual admissions offers many avenues for close cooperation between the community college and the transfer college, especially where the two institutions are relatively close together geographically. At a community college, and at the upper division–graduate branch campus of a land-grant state university in Pennsylvania twenty minutes away, dual admissions has brought about the introduction of complementary programs and services. A baccalaureate criminal justice program tailored to the community college curriculum guaranteed associate degree recipients the opportunity for upper-division work and a baccalaureate degree in their field. The two faculties who worked closely on the curriculum continuum now have a vested interest in promoting each other's offerings and institutions.

The community college had strong and varied technology programs supported by state-of-the-art equipment. The transfer college strengthened its standard physics and other related science courses to offer a bachelor of technology degree. The advantage to the community college was that its career graduates now had the option of transfer and an opportunity to work for a baccalaureate degree that offered career enhancement.

The close cooperation has also led increasing numbers of community college faculty to take graduate courses. In this case, the transfer college added a doctoral program in adult education that is proving increasingly attractive to two-year faculty for professional growth and development.

Cultural programs and library holdings can also be shared. Students and staff can be offered reciprocal tickets to events. The colleges can share artists-in-residence or share arts faculty. They can share periodicals, which, while educationally necessary, may not be greatly in demand. Community college students gain access to a good research collection, while students at the transfer college gain access to specialized, curriculum-specific holdings.

In the present example, the colleges share the high costs of video instruction. The public-access cable channel is located on the community college campus, but cable time is divided equally. Each campus has an electronic classroom linked by microwave so that each campus can originate its own programs on the shared channel. The agreement governing the operation of the access channel restricts the range of video credit courses that each college can offer along lower division–upper division lines, but it does not restrict competition in the noncredit area.

A narrowcast channel connecting twenty-two business and industrial firms to the network has been jointly developed in conjunction with a local television station. Each campus controls its own job development video offerings, and a video series on the state's new chemical right-to-know legislation was developed in partnership.

Cooperative faculty exchanges and professional development sessions have been extremely successful. Each faculty serves to stimulate the other by widening the pool of scholars and increasing academic interaction and exchange. The combination of two budgets makes it possible to obtain expensive external talent as guest speakers. The increased audience helps to attract talented resource people. Faculty exchanges can range from guest lecturing to scholars-in-residence, including scholars from abroad. The community college served as host for a Chinese professor-in-residence and provided office space and housing. The transfer college used its ability to issue the IAP-66 form to secure the necessary visa. Thus, the visiting scholar was jointly sponsored, and each campus enjoyed the benefits of cultural exchange.

Campus housing represents another area of cooperation. Many community college students come from distant communities. Unused student housing at the transfer college has been made available to them. Commuting time for the students has been reduced, and occupancy at the university's dormitory has increased.

Dual Admissions with Other Colleges

In addition to its dual admissions arrangements with nearby institutions, the community college just described has a dual admissions relationship with six traditionally black private colleges belonging to the United Negro College Fund (UNCF). In this case, the UNCF acted as a broker by identifying six institutions that were interested in participating in a pilot project aimed at increasing black enrollment in higher education and persistence to a baccalaureate degree. The community college hosted a meeting that brought staff from the six participating transfer institutions together. This meeting had been preceded by community college staff visits to the six institutions. A grant from the Fund for the Improvement of Post-Secondary Education helps to foster faculty exchanges and provides assistance in assessments and workshops. A designated counselor at the community college is responsible for coordinating student recruitment. Special admissions materials, including videotapes of the participating colleges, have been planned to acquaint local students with the six transfer colleges. The transfer colleges agree to house high school students who wish to visit their campuses at no charge. As a result, black and other high school students now have options they might otherwise have missed.

Conclusion

Pennsylvania's system of higher education consists of fourteen community colleges, fourteen state universities, the Pennsylvania State University, University of Pittsburgh, Temple University, and a number of private two- and four-year colleges. Richly divergent and pluralistic, the system has no strong state coordinating agency. Each institution has been relatively autonomous in developing its mission, in reaching out to identified constituencies, and in seeking alliances with sister institutions. Flexibility has been maximized, and constraint has been minimized.

Within this context, cooperation and conciliation have usually prevailed over narrow parochialism, and the student has emerged as the winner. Articulation between junior- and senior-level colleges based on degree integrity, equity, dual admissions, and interinstitutional cooperation has helped to enhance educational opportunities for citizens, curtail unnecessary duplication of programs and services, improve relations between the various segments of higher education, and preserve the plurality and diversity of colleges and universities.

Kenneth B. Woodbury, Jr., is president of Harrisburg Area Community College in Pennsylvania.

In Florida, articulation among high schools, colleges, and universities goes far beyond courses for transfer, dealing as it does with all aspects of education, including facilities, data gathering, resources, and systemwide philosophy of higher education.

Articulation Florida Style

Robert S. Palinchak

Articulation Florida style is unique to institutions of higher learning, in particular to community colleges. In contrast to states that have allowed tradition and custom to isolate venerable institutions, Florida is relatively new to higher education and relatively unfettered with elitism and blind tradition. Indeed, Florida's newness and inexperience keep it relatively free of the external influences that challenge its far-reaching articulation concepts in other states.

Systems Approach

Florida's system of postsecondary education consists of nine universities and twenty-eight community colleges. Vocational-technical (vo-tech) centers are active components of only half of the community colleges; thirty-three other postsecondary vocational centers are controlled by local school boards.

The 2+2 concept is an important element of Florida's articulation history. Under the 2+2 concept, the twenty-eight two-year junior colleges serve as feeder institutions for the nine universities, the majority of which were conceived and built as two-year upper-level institutions designed primarily to receive lower-division students. Thus, the need for one sector or division to "fit" into or upon another was paramount from the start. The 2+2 design called for university-parallel courses to be offered exclu-

C. Prager (ed.). *Enhancing Articulation and Transfer.*
New Directions for Community Colleges, no. 61. San Francisco: Jossey-Bass, Spring 1988.

sively at the lower level. Originally, only Florida State, the University of Florida, and Florida A & M University were to teach their own freshmen and sophomores.

Unforeseen circumstances prevented the 2+2 plan from being implemented as designed. For one thing, increasing numbers of students demanded vocationalism in the curriculum, which led to an emphasis on associate in science and associate in applied science degree programs. Florida has always viewed the A.S. degree as a terminal degree with job emphasis, and it has never recognized the A.A.S. in rule or in law.

The universities recently won the right to full four-year curricula, so that the concept of the university as an exclusively upper-level institution is now defunct. Vo-tech schools grant vocational credit that can be applied toward appropriate degrees, although the schools themselves cannot award college credit or degrees. Thus, there is an evident need for articulation among the various sectors that now exist in Florida: K–12, with its thirty-three postsecondary vo-tech centers; the twenty-eight community colleges, with their fourteen integrated vo-tech centers; and the universities, which may, but generally do not, grant the associate degree. The need for articulation was evident from the start. States where the need is not so pressing may arrive at the point of articulation later in their development and adopt different formats.

Governance and State Coordination of Sectors

The K–12 sector is governed by locally elected school boards, the community college sector has three years of experience under a relatively new state board of community colleges appointed by the governor, and the state university system is governed by a board of regents whose members are appointed by the governor. Clearly, the need for articulation is present even at the highest levels. The boards, which employ an executive director and a chancellor, respectively, work under the general authority of the Florida State Board of Education, which is composed of the Florida cabinet, including the governor and the commissioner of education.

The Postsecondary Education Planning Commission. The Postsecondary Education Planning Commission (PEPC), which was initiated by the governor's office but has been befriended by the legislature, oversees plans and studies affecting all present and future education in Florida. Its range of influence, control, and support is enormous, as is its overriding mission to achieve a systematic approach by maximizing the use of limited resources. Through the PEPC, the governor and the legislature have imposed a philosophy and a mechanism that call for a focused view of education and a systems approach wherein each sector is dovetailed and interdependent with the other sectors.

The reader needs to remember that Florida's postsecondary system is essentially of recent vintage and that it came into existence as a result of calls for effectiveness, efficiency, and, most important, universal availability to an extremely diverse clientele in a large, rapidly growing, and changing state. Despite or perhaps because of contradictions in its brief but episodic growth, the system has felt the need for coordination and articulation from the very start. Access and planning have been hallmarks of the Florida system for some time. So, too, is political influence, especially from the top down.

Legislative Influence. One of the hallmarks of education in Southern states is heavy political involvement in the details of educational affairs. While this is not unusual in present times, it characterized the South long before funding and education became as closely entwined as they are today. Florida also embraced vocationalism and its concomitant funding network, as did many midwestern and western states.

Owing either to the sheer size of the state or to the strong internal interest in selective aspects of education, the legislature has long desired to coordinate services and agencies. Both houses have the extensive staff and resources needed to pull together and disseminate information. Special legislature committees give high priority to funding, capital outlay, and general appropriations, which all affect education. Primarily through the strong influence of staff and advisory committees, the legislature regularly involves itself in the most minute details of schooling, including number of periods in a day, number of words in required compositions, testing, and curriculum. Day-to-day legislative involvement is compounded by judicial influence and fear of litigation. It is not unusual for a high school superintendent or a college president to be surveyed directly by the senate appropriations committee or the governor's office on educational affairs. Lobbying is intense, and educational dollars are significant.

The Articulation Rule and Committee

The Articulation Agreement, Rule 6A-10.024 of the Florida Administrative Code, formally established articulation requirements between and among universities, community colleges, and school districts in 1973. It calls for each university president, community college, and school board to provide articulated programs that enable students to proceed toward educational objectives as rapidly as their circumstances permit. The rule calls for written procedures, accelerating mechanisms, exchange of ideas, and improvement of programs of general education. While the original mandate was simply to facilitate the transfer of students from the colleges to the universities, the breadth and depth of the mission has led to the development of a number of creative mechanisms and arrangements.

The twelve-member state Articulation Coordinating Committee is appointed by the commissioner of education. Three members apiece represent the state university system, the community college system, and public schools, and one represents vocational education. A member from the commissioner's staff serves as chairperson, and there is one additional member.

Under rule, the committee accepts continuous responsibility for university-community college-school district relationships. It hears cases or appeals from students who have encountered difficulty in transferring. While the committee's decisions are advisory, systemwide issues covering all sectors are openly discussed. This process does not preclude contact between and among academic faculty and departments, which often meet to discuss similar matters of local or regional concern.

The Articulation Coordinating Committee is charged with distinguishing lower-level from upper-level courses, and it reviews general education courses, introductory courses, first courses, and general survey courses. It levels postsecondary vocational and adult vocational programs or assigns them to the appropriate sector, basing its decisions on such considerations as job entry preparation, theoretical versus practical instruction, and licensing or accrediting requirements pertinent to the associate degree. The desire to produce uniform classification is an indirect response to the questionable place of vo-tech centers among Florida's high schools and community colleges.

The rule calls for specific review of such issues as academic record forms, general education requirements, units of credit, course numbering systems, grading systems, calendars, and credit by examination. As a result, a plethora of inquiries and studies is continually under way, sometimes complementary, often in opposition, but always in pursuit of improved linkages among all educational institutions.

Effects of the Articulation Rule on Transfer

Florida's articulation rule calls for all public institutions of higher education to recognize the integrity of one another's general education programs. The basic program for students seeking the baccalaureate degree involves not less than thirty-six semester hours of credit. Once a student has been certified as having satisfactorily completed such a program, no other public college or university is to require additional lower-division general education courses of the student.

For the sixty-credit-hour Associate in Arts degree, thirty-six semester hours are required, with not less than a 2.0 average in all courses attempted. (Only the last grade received enters into the calculations for a repeated course.) However, each university has discretion to accept or reject the grade of D in the major.

Actual admission to an upper-level program is often competitive due to space and cost considerations. Currently, senior institutions base their evaluations of associate degrees other than the A.A. degree on the applicability of the courses to the baccalaureate major. Vocational credit earned from any vo-tech center or academic credit from any public community college or university must be awarded credit by the receiving institution, if the credit is judged to be equivalent under the statewide common course-numbering system.

The state mandates consistency in the numbering of similar courses so that a course with a given number has common goals and objectives and has similar expectations for students wherever it is taught. Faculty have very mixed views of this concept and its effectiveness.

A study is currently under way to determine what protection can be offered for courses not covered by the articulation agreement. Now, credit is protected only for community college courses offered by the receiving university.

In reality, increasing numbers of students are choosing to transfer without the A.A. degree. Many transfer with the A.S. or with only a common core of general education courses. If this tendency is viewed positively, the system will adjust to it and in some manner legitimize it.

Effect of the Articulation Rule on Community Colleges and High Schools

The articulation rule requires community college presidents to file annual articulation plans. Parents are to be made aware of definitions, opportunities, and joint ventures. High school faculty who can teach college courses in high schools are to be identified, and the course offerings of high schools and colleges are to be coordinated in order to prevent unnecessary duplication. Community college courses are to be complementary to the high school curriculum. Community college presidents are also required to prepare annual evaluation reports indicating numbers and percentage of students participating by high school, student performance, hours of participation at college levels within the high schools, and so forth. Annual instructional materials agreements are worked out with school districts for dual enrollment programs. These agreements facilitate reimbursement to colleges for materials used or consumed by high school students in dual enrollment programs authorized by the legislature.

Other Extensions of the Articulation Rule

Under the 1982 General Appropriations Act, the Articulating Coordinating Committee was asked to define full-time-equivalent (FTE) terms, such as *credit, college credit, vocational credit, noncredit, developmental credit,* and *college preparatory credit.* Much of the push in this direction has come from vocational forces seeking equivalency in the postsecondary or higher education marketplace.

At the present time, the Articulation Coordinating Committee is helping to codify the appropriate level for specific courses or programs to be offered. Criteria are being developed to show the intended level for baccalaureate, postsecondary vocational, and postsecondary adult vocational offerings. The process is simplistic and highly politicized. Vocational interests appear to be promoting it as a means of precluding duplication. Some see it as protection of turf and contrary to the best interests of higher education in Florida.

In addition to course numbering, articulation ensures common calendars, common high school and college transcripts, common test dates, and common data analysis for student grades and state reports. Through a combination of rule, law, and agency directive, representative committees develop guidelines, which are circulated and generally adhered to in a positive working fashion.

The articulation committee works closely with administrators of the College-Level Academic Skills Program (CLASP) and the College-Level Academic Skills Test (CLAST) to ensure coordination of testing, score reporting, and so forth. At present, each sophomore is required to pass CLAST before receiving an A.A. degree or becoming a junior at the state university. This program has been effective in elevating Florida's academic standards. Unfortunately, the program was put in place by legislators, not by educators.

Minimal standards for foreign language requirements set by the legislature, and higher standards desired by some universities for the baccalaureate, are being studied. The natural involvement of high schools and community colleges in the study is a hallmark of Florida articulation.

The Independent Articulation Agreement Feasibility Study revealed that Florida's independent colleges had no interest in setting up or participating in a comprehensive articulation program. In contrast to the Northeast, for example, Florida does not have many fiercely independent colleges, nor does it have the quantity of prestigious private, independent, or church-related colleges that in other states might make articulation both more urgent and more difficult. To date, they deem individual school-to-school plans sufficient.

The Student On-Line Advisement and Articulation System (SOLAR) is intended to enhance and strengthen articulation among high schools, colleges, and universities through technology. Now under development, SOLAR is one of the most elaborate undertakings ever envisioned as part of an articulation procedure. SOLAR is designed to complement the state university's Student Academic Support System

(SASS). Supported by appropriate legislative enactment, including fiscal and other resources, its goal is a statewide computer-assisted student advising network.

SOLAR will provide specialized information to transfer students, including information about transfer procedures, admissions requirements, and special course requirements for special university majors. The system will also provide feedback on student progress in various majors and compare it with progress by students in other majors and disciplines at other Florida colleges. It will show trends and tendencies for compliance with or deviance from established norms due to problems associated with transfer, prerequisites, grades, completion time, repeated courses, progress rates, completion rates, and grade point averages throughout the entire state university system.

The Florida Information and Resource Network (FIRN) is being developed to connect all educational institutions in the state with Tallahassee. It will use data banks and computers to facilitate information exchange on a statewide level in any area of operation. All public schools and colleges will be connected for the sharing and coordination of data. Some fear that this network will make the legislature a statewide school board.

Articulation, a regular publication of the state department of education, provides course information statewide. Grade point averages are indicated for each university by major field or college as a means of comparison. In general, this summary of institutional academic standing is well received, respected, and well read.

Future of Florida's Articulation System

The services, directives, studies, and reports just described vary greatly in quality and effectiveness. They are often far too quantitative and excessively grounded in management techniques. The system of articulation sometimes seems to consist of unconnected doctoral studies and variant staff reports. Many of these products are immediately transformed into legislative mandate, then delayed or not funded. Others are applied inequitably or in twenty-eight different ways, thus weakening any effective study of comparability. Still, a caring and sharing system is clearly better than a system in which disinterest or distrust is symptomatic of poor cooperation among institutions of higher learning or of poor relationships between institutions and external governing or coordinating authorities. In contrast to states that leave individual students to fend for themselves, Florida has taken positive steps toward articulation.

Clearly, statewide articulation and coordination are well under way. Extending far beyond the primary concern for transfer students, the concept is now reaching out into common reports, coordinated computers, integrated software, common data banks, sharing of resources, and joint facilities.

Joint Facilities and Shared Resources. The state's desire to promote effective use of limited resources encourages joint facilities, dual enrollments, sharing of faculty, exchange of personnel, minisabbaticals, joint programs with business and industry, matching grants, business linkages, and shared use of facilities. It is not at all uncommon for a county civic center to be built in conjunction with a community college or for a community college campus building to be developed for shared use by the regional university. A high school–community college is erected to meet the needs of a growing school district in the vicinity of a growing community college, or a major arts center is built on the community college site, in concert with the local state university.

A Local Example: Lake-Sumter's Nursing Program. Lake-Sumter Community College is a small institution of approximately 1,000 full-time equivalent students, about thirty miles north of Orlando. Primarily transfer-oriented, the college has slowly incorporated vocational courses and programs in order to produce a balanced curriculum. By developing strong linkages with the immediate community, the college was able to initiate a one-year bridge program to train registered nurses (RNs). Participants were required to have one year of experience as a licensed practical nurse (LPN) in order to finish in one year. The college also offers a standard two-year program culminating in eligibility for RN licensure and the A.S. degree.

Local hospitals have contributed significant financial support over the past five years, and they will continue to do so. This support will lead the University of Central Florida to offer bachelor of science in nursing (BSN) programs through the community college on a cooperating basis. It appears that the M.S. in nursing may also be offered, with additional in-service and continuing education courses. In all cases, nursing education will take place in joint-use facilities with shared faculty.

Accelerated Articulation. As broad as the concept of articulation now appears to be, the underlying theory is about to undergo an even broader application. An accelerated articulation bill was one of the first to be presented to the legislature in 1987. It exempted students from dual enrollment fees, required free instructional materials for dual enrollment, established special funding for dual enrollment, required community colleges to offer credit by examination, required school superintendents and community college presidents to establish articulation agreements, authorized advanced placement courses and funding, exempted certain secondary students from certain community college admission requirements, and required PEPC to study funding formulas for certain accelerated articulation programs. Again, the Florida concept of articulation is extended by legislative mandate.

Articulation in the Broadest Sense

The original aim of Florida's articulation concept was to help community college students to transfer. Florida now articulates or coordinates nearly every aspect of its educational enterprise. School boards meet with college trustees; high school teachers meet with their counterparts at the college level. The governor and the legislature encourage dual enrollment and early admission practices. The state wants college courses to be taught in the high schools; it also wants faculty exchange and resource sharing where feasible.

To be sure, there are some concerns that commonality will produce mediocrity. Faculty argue the notion of common course numbering and legislative directions on class size (twenty-two for basic mathematics and English) and writing requirements for basic English (at least 6,000 words per semester). Some joint facilities turn out to be less than disinterested legislative projects. A common computer system to formulate a giant data base for all institutions gives the legislature a Big Brother image for those who perceive the project as efficient but not effective. The leveling of vocational-technical curricula by committee eliminates any uniqueness that might have developed. Some are troubled by the pride taken in the notion that a student or course has been taught at the lowest, quickest, least expensive level possible.

While other states permit students to graduate who may not be accepted by a senior institution or, worse yet, force students to negotiate acceptance on a course-by-course basis, Florida has an articulation system that responds to students' needs. Indeed, students are the clear winners in Florida's broadly applied articulation concepts.

With moderation and common sense, articulation Florida style will prove effective. It will also provide a model for other states to emulate or to use as a basis in developing their own versions of articulation.

Robert S. Palinchak is president of Lake-Sumter Community College in Leesburg, Florida.

Discrepancies in articulation policies and practice in the liberal arts and sciences lead to inconsistencies and confusion in the transfer of community college courses to senior college baccalaureate programs.

Transferability in the Liberal Arts and Sciences

Dympna Bowles

Since the rise of community colleges in the 1950s, policies to improve articulation in the liberal arts and sciences have been promulgated in states and university systems nationwide as a means of increasing the educational access and mobility of community college students. These policies generally address the transferability of community college credit for liberal arts associate degree graduates and stipulate a minimum number of credits to be transferred to senior colleges. For example, Florida's General Education Compact specifies that thirty-six credits in general education course work can be applied toward the baccalaureate degree in the state's public universities (Florida Department of Education, 1971). New Jersey's full faith in credit policy mandates that all public state colleges award credit for general education courses that are part of the transfer degree programs of community colleges (New Jersey Board of Higher Education, 1981). In California, each community college specifies what it regards as baccalaureate-appropriate courses that public state colleges accept as transferable (Office of the Chancellor, 1973). The underlying goal of these policies is to ensure that community college students do not accumulate an excessive number of credits on their route to the baccalaureate degree.

While such policies represent broad institutional commitments

C. Prager (ed.). *Enhancing Articulation and Transfer.*
New Directions for Community Colleges, no. 61. San Francisco: Jossey-Bass, Spring 1988.

to the advancement of the educational mobility of community college students, the implementation of such policies is often problematic. Richardson and Bender's (1985) study of articulation and transfer in public urban university systems documents an uneven record of accomplishment when transfer policies are actually implemented. These authors conclude that the award of transfer credit is in worse shape today than it was a decade ago and that senior colleges have become less willing to accept courses and grades earned in community colleges. The differing missions and traditions of senior and community colleges, the entry of large numbers of underprepared students through open-admissions programs, the rise of careerism, and changes in degree aspirations among students enrolled in nominally terminal career programs account for much of the difficulty in assessing the transferability of liberal arts courses to senior college programs. These developments have complicated the assessment of community college courses and compounded curricular issues that already exist in the transfer of community college liberal arts courses.

Without systematic efforts to address legitimate curricular issues relevant to transferability, policies that only mandate compliance create confusion, and in the long run they are ineffective. When senior colleges feel coerced by policy to accept community college courses that they view as inappropriate, they often devise alternative strategies that impede efforts to improve articulation. These strategies include the imposition of stringent measures to assess student competence, such as requiring specific grades in courses or requiring students to pass validation examinations (Richardson and Bender, 1985). If the transferability of community college courses is to improve, a series of well-developed policies must be accompanied by systematic and cooperative strategies designed to address legitimate curricular issues. In systems and states where this occurs, such as Florida and California, articulation is much more firmly rooted and much more effective.

At the City University of New York (CUNY), a public university system that includes nine senior and seven community colleges, articulation policies governing transfer of credit in the liberal arts have been promulgated since the early 1970s. These policies guarantee a place for CUNY associate in arts (A.A.) and associate in science (A.S.) degree graduates in one of the system's senior colleges (Board of Trustees, 1972). In addition, they place an upper limit of sixty-four on the number of credits that the senior colleges of CUNY can require of A.A. and A.S. graduates. A related policy requires that community college graduates with the associate in applied science (A.A.S.) degree who transfer into a related senior college professional program or a liberal arts curriculum cannot be required to take more than seventy-two credits at the senior college (Board of Trustees, 1973). A more recent policy on articulation in the liberal arts and sciences stipulates the full transferability of all liberal arts and sciences courses to senior colleges throughout the system (Board of Trustees, 1985). While these policies are coherent and well intentioned, and while they point the way toward improved articulation, the implementation of these policies has been uneven within the system. In a number of cases, students have accumulated in excess of 128 credits for the baccalaureate degree. Given CUNY's stated mission of access and excellence and the disproportionate number of minority students enrolled in its community colleges, such discrepancies between policy and practice are disturbing.

As a first step toward improving the transferability of credit, CUNY's central office of Academic Affairs began two major initiatives: first, the compilation of comprehensive information on the transferability of community college courses to each of the ten senior colleges in the system; second, the formation of faculty-based articulation task forces to address problems and issues in specific disciplines in the liberal arts and sciences. These systemwide activities complement a variety of campus-based initiatives already under way at a number of CUNY colleges, including the development of college-to-college articulation agreements as well as special transfer projects at three of CUNY's community colleges—Bronx, Hostos, and LaGuardia—funded under the Ford Foundation's Urban Community College Transfer Opportunities Program. Chapter Four in this volume describes the project at Hostos.

Systemwide Course Equivalency Information

The absence of comprehensive information on the transferability of community college liberal arts courses to the senior colleges in the system has been a major problem for CUNY's transfer students. Despite persistent complaints regarding the transfer of credit for these courses, there was little documentation on the ways in which these courses were evaluated by the senior colleges in the system. Thus, it was not clear to what extent and in what ways the university's transfer policies had been implemented. More important, because students did not have this transferability information, they were unable to plan their academic programs early enough to avoid unnecessary duplication of course work and loss of community college credit. To remedy this situation, the university, with the assistance of the Ford Foundation, compiled a guide (Bowles, 1985) containing senior college evaluations of community college courses.

Senior College Evaluations of Community College Courses. The guide contains evaluations of all 3,768 community college courses by each of the system's ten senior colleges—a total of 37,680 evaluations. Table 1 presents the results of these evaluations by category and type of course.

Table 1. Senior College Evaluations of Community College Courses by Evaluation Category and Type of Course

	Type of Course					
	Liberal Arts		*Career*		*Total*	
Evaluation Category	*Number*	*%*	*Number*	*%*	*Number*	*%*
Transferable						
Equivalent	12,252	53	2,892	20	15,144	40
Elective: Meets specific degree requirements	2,353	10	434	3	2,787	7
Elective: Does not meet degree requirements	6,150	27	3,599	25	9,749	26
Total Transferable	20,755	90	6,925	48	27,680	73
Not Transferable	1,938	8	7,375	51	9,313	25
Not Evaluated	457	2	230	2	687	2
Total Evaluations	23,150	100	14,430	100	37,680	100

Overall, 73 percent of the senior college evaluations identify community college courses as transferable to senior colleges in the university and 25 percent as not transferable. Approximately 47 percent of the evaluations identify courses as meeting degree requirements at the senior colleges, with 40 percent as direct equivalents and 7 percent as meeting specific distribution or core requirements or requirements in the major. Twenty-six percent of the evaluations identify courses as free electives that, while technically transferable to the senior college, do not fulfill requirements for the baccalaureate degree. A full 25 percent of the evaluations identify courses as not transferable to the senior college.

Liberal Arts and Career-Oriented Courses. To determine more specifically which courses received what kind of evaluations, an analysis was made of liberal arts and career-oriented courses. Community college courses were broadly categorized as liberal arts or as career-oriented courses by the department or program under which they were listed in the community college catalogue. While such a categorization is by no means exact, it nevertheless provides a means of making broad distinctions at the course level. Almost 90 percent of the liberal arts and science evaluations identify community college courses as transferable, compared to 48 percent for the career-oriented courses. Only 10 percent of the liberal arts courses were evaluated as not transferable, compared to approximately 51 percent of the career-oriented courses. Further, 63 percent of the liberal arts courses met degree requirements, and more than four fifths of these were judged direct equivalents, whereas only 23 percent of the professional courses fulfilled such requirements at the senior college. For both kinds of courses, almost the same proportion, one fourth, was identified as free electives.

While career courses continue to encounter serious problems in transferability, there are sufficient difficulties with liberal arts courses to justify concern. A full 35 percent of all liberal arts and science courses are either in the free elective or not transferable categories and hence not applicable to the baccalaureate degree. These results are supported by an audit of transcripts of CUNY community college liberal arts graduates, which found that 24 percent of these graduates were awarded fewer than sixty-four credits toward the baccalaureate degree, with a range of twenty to sixty-three credits applied to the degree (Office of Academic Affairs, 1987a). The evaluations in the guide (Bowles, 1985) and the results of the audit together provide concrete evidence that the university's articulation policies in the liberal arts and sciences have not been implemented fully—a finding that is disturbing, given the prevailing assumption that liberal arts courses pose little difficulty in transfer.

Faculty Articulation Task Forces

In an effort to explore the reasons for these transfer-of-credit problems and address them systematically, the university established a series of faculty-based articulation task forces in the liberal arts and sciences (Office of Academic Affairs, 1987b). Because the assessment of community college courses in the guide (Bowles, 1985) was largely a unilateral process, with senior colleges determining the evaluations, it was important for the university's next step toward the improvement of articulation to be a collaborative one that involved faculty from both community and senior colleges. For this reason, each task force was composed of a faculty member from each of the seventeen colleges in the City University system, and each task force was co-chaired by a faculty member from a senior college and a faculty member from a community college.

Five task forces representing three broad divisions in the liberal arts—the humanities, the social sciences, and the sciences—were formed in biology, chemistry, English, mathematics, and psychology. Each task force was charged with identifying problems and issues in the transfer of credit within the discipline and with making recommendations for resolving them. The task forces were staffed by members of the Office of Academic Affairs, who provided the administrative and logistical support required. Besides taking care of the administrative details, central office staff provided a university perspective where relevant. The task forces met four times over a five-month period in 1987 and examined course syllabi, exams, and required readings from the seventeen colleges in the system. They formed subcommittees to address a number of problems, which fell into two broad categories: curricular problems relating to transfer of credit within the discipline and college and systemwide communication problems impeding effective articulation throughout the university. The next two sections address task force findings in these two areas.

Curricular Problems in Transfer of Credit

Difficulties in the transfer of liberal arts courses arise largely because of discrepancies in content, scope, and level between senior college and community college courses. In general, if a community college course is not a mirror image of a course at the senior college, if it does not "fit" into senior college requirements, or if it is taught at a lower level than it is at the senior college, the practice is to award it elective credit that is usually not applied toward the baccalaureate degree. Special difficulties arise with the liberal arts "service" courses offered in career programs and with basic skills courses in reading, writing, and mathematics. Courses in the second category account for a large part of the liberal arts and science courses that are not applied to the baccalaureate degree.

Discrepancies in Content and Scope. Standard, traditional liberal arts courses, such as "Introduction to Psychology," "Calculus," and "General Biology," generally do not encounter difficulty in being transferred and usually receive the best evaluation—that is, as direct equivalents. Because these courses are similar in content, scope, and perspective to courses offered at the senior college, they fit neatly into the overall curricular sequence of the particular baccalaureate program. Any problems that arise in the transfer of such courses are usually the result of some deviation from the expected pattern. For example, a course is part of a sequence, and the student transfers without completing the entire sequence. This kind of problem occurs most often in mathematics and the sciences. Since the treatment of topics within a community college and a senior college course sequence often varies, the community college course has no corresponding match or equivalent at the senior college, and the course is evaluated as a free elective. A related source of difficulty arises when a community college course, in addressing the needs of its students, covers in two semesters what the senior college course covers in one. The resulting discrepancy in course credit leads the course to be evaluated as a free elective.

Interdisciplinary liberal arts courses offered by the community colleges also encounter transfer-of-credit problems, since they usually reflect new and creative arrangements of knowledge that differ from the traditional liberal arts courses offered by a senior college. Such courses as

"Humanism and Technology," "Biology and the Law," and "Art, Politics, and Protest," which do not appear to match traditional curricular offerings, are often not evaluated as direct equivalents or as fulfilling degree requirements at the senior college. The diversity of missions, goals, and curricula precludes an exact fit of courses and programs. For example, variation in course content, sequence, and level can be observed even in a single course taught within the same senior college department. Further complications arise when a senior college has developed a core curriculum in which newly designed interdisciplinary courses differ markedly from traditional courses. Such courses as "Science in Modern Life: Chemistry and Physics" and "Introduction to Mathematical Reasoning and Computer Programming," which reflect unique combinations of disciplines, would have difficulty being articulated even into a traditional senior college program. Yet, because the transfer process is driven largely by the senior colleges, such creativity and ingenuity on the part of the community colleges is often unrewarded—indeed, it is often penalized—during the transfer process.

If students are to be treated fairly and the transfer process is to become rational, faculties must move beyond the concept of equivalence or exact fit to a more flexible standard of evaluation. At the same time, flexibility should not compromise academic quality and standards. Reasonable efforts should be made to determine whether courses that do not fit can be applied to the major or to general education or distribution or core requirements. In some instances, community college courses may fit under a special-topics rubric; in others, students should have the option of demonstrating mastery of content by taking an exam, rather than having to repeat related course work. In cases where a course is part of a sequence, students should be advised to complete the entire sequence before transferring in order to reduce the number of "lost" credits.

Discrepancies in Level and Prerequisites. Problems of transferability become most pronounced when there are differences in course standards, levels, and prerequisites. The entry of large numbers of underprepared students into the university through open admissions has highlighted the importance of maintaining program standards and quality. Concern with issues of standards is most obvious in mathematics and the sciences, where the acquisition of knowledge and skills is presumed to occur in a hierarchical dovetailing fashion. As a result, in such courses as calculus or introductory laboratory science, prerequisites are stringently set, and students are required to meet them before moving on to courses at the next level. Because community college courses are designed to meet the needs of students who are less academically prepared on entry than their counterparts in four-year colleges, the level of some of the basic courses is often lower, and course prerequisites are less rigorous. As a result, faculty in four-year colleges submit examinations and assignments to close scrutiny in order to determine course level, or else they require students to pass validation exams. In some cases, the resulting treatment accorded to transfer students is inequitable when compared with the treatment accorded to resident four-year students, who are usually not required to demonstrate their competence once they have passed a course.

Given that students learn in a variety of ways and that the acquisition of concepts may not be so discrete a process as such practices assume, it is important to differentiate between prerequisites that are fundamental and prerequisites that may be generally desirable but are not essential. It may be that the acquisition of concepts in mathematics and the sciences less resembles a strictly vertical and linear arrangement than it does a spiral, where one learns at different points and in different ways. To paraphrase a faculty member of the biology task force, the acquisition of knowledge in biology may be less like a linear path with discrete steps, specific prerequisities, and strict course sequencing than it is like a mosaic with branching and rebranching and multiple prerequisites (Graham, 1987). Since such a view challenges long-established notions of how knowledge is acquired, resolving discrepancies in course level and prerequisites will require creative and ingenious approaches to transfer of credit on the part of both community and senior college faculty.

Liberal Arts Courses in Career-Oriented Programs. Perhaps the most problematic issue is the transfer of liberal arts courses that function as service courses in career programs leading to A.A.S. degrees. For example, a biology course within a dental hygiene program and a mathematics course for students in a health science program typify courses that pose special problems for transfer. In meeting the curricular needs of students in career programs, these service courses often include material that is vocational or applied. For example, a microbiology course may focus on the laboratory techniques that are required for a job but that are not often included in "pure" or "hard" microbiology courses for liberal arts students. Because of its vocational emphasis, such a course is usually seen as a free elective or as not transferable.

The increasing vocationalism of the university's students complicates the transfer of such liberal arts service courses. Approximately 80 percent of community college graduates obtain the associate degree in career areas (Office of Institutional Research, 1985). While the applied orientation of these courses creates problems in transferability, dismissing such courses out of hand, with no regard for the kinds of thinking and knowledge taught in them or for their possible benefits, does a disservice to students. Some of the best instruction uses a combination of theory and practice, and the vocational focus of these service courses may provide a bridge to the more abstract concepts taught in the hard sciences. The negative impact of the career umbrella can be seen in the stringent evaluation accorded to traditional liberal arts courses that, while housed in a career program, are identical to traditional courses for liberal arts students. As a member of the biology task force put it (Graham, 1987), the taint of the medical technology frame often affects the evaluation of such courses negatively. Assessing the benefits of such liberal arts service courses is thus a challenging task. Nevertheless, it will provide faculty with new ways of looking at the relation between liberal arts and career areas.

Basic Skills Courses. Many of the liberal arts courses that receive the "not transferable" designation are basic courses in reading, writing, and mathematics. These courses include both credit and noncredit courses, such as "Reading and Study Skills," "Intensive Writing," and "Elementary Algebra," as well as many courses in English as a second language. These courses are designed to enable students to develop proficiency in the basic skills and to meet the CUNY minimum skills requirement before moving on to the university's upper division. Remedial skills courses are offered in both the senior and the community colleges. Approximately 85 percent of the freshmen in the community colleges and 67 percent of the freshmen in the senior colleges enroll in at least one of them (Office of Institutional Research, 1985). The courses offered in these two settings often cover the same topics and competencies, but because the senior colleges have higher admissions standards, they often do not consider community college skills courses to be comparable to their own. Thus, whether community college basic courses are credit or noncredit, they are generally evaluated as not transferable to the senior colleges.

Problems of transferability are complicated by the need for assessing and placing students in writing. The English task force focused largely on issues related to the evaluation of community college students' writing competence and to their placement within the appropriate senior college writing sequence. A major complication arises when students have passed basic courses in the community colleges but have not met the university's minimum skills requirement by passing the CUNY assessment test. These students generally are retested by the senior colleges, and, if they fail, they are placed in the senior college basic skills sequence, although they may already have passed a similar course at the community college. This practice often creates morale problems for students who do not pass when retested and must enroll in skills courses that are similar in many ways to the courses they took and passed at the community college.

In addressing this issue, the English task force recommended that criteria and procedures for evaluation and placement should consider both test scores and courses completed so that transfer students' prior work is not ignored. Further, it recommended that transfer and native students be treated equitably with regard to assessment and placement procedures. Examples of inequitable treatment exist in a number of CUNY colleges. In some instances, a student must demonstrate mastery by passing a so-called validation exam before enrolling in a course at the next level. In other cases, the student must earn a specific grade in the course in order to receive equivalent credit. Such differential treatment should be avoided if the same requirements do not apply to resident students. For example, once course equivalence has been established, no further mastery of material should be required of transfer students that is not required of resident students. Further, grades from senior and community colleges should be treated equally, and criteria for the evaluation of writing should be the same for transfer and for resident students. However, it is important to separate unfair practices from practices that appear to be discriminatory only as a result of lack of information on current procedures at the senior colleges. In some cases, what is perceived to be inequitable treatment turns out to involve requirements that are applied to resident senior college students as well. This fact highlights the importance of accurate and timely systemwide information on requirements and procedures that affect transfer students.

The Need for Improved Information and Communication

Many of the articulation problems that the task forces identified stem from poor information and communication between and among the CUNY colleges. In particular, there is a notable absence of essential systemwide information on degree and major requirements, courses, and syllabi and on policies and procedures for testing and placement. In attempting to address these issues, a number of task forces entertained the possibility of developing common, universitywide standards of transferability in specific liberal arts and science disciplines. For example, the chemistry task force discussed the idea of using the American Chemical Association test for proficiency in basic chemistry, and the mathematics task force discussed the feasibility of developing a universitywide test in precalculus. However, given the size, diversity, and autonomy of the university's colleges, it soon became clear that attempts to mandate uniform requirements in the system were at best complicated and time-consuming and at worst overly prescriptive and doomed to failure. Rather, improved communication and information among academic departments would provide a more effective way of improving transferability. Roughly half of the task forces' eighty-five recommendations addressed the need for better information and communication as a way of improving the transferability of liberal arts courses. Effective articulation is possible only if and when a high priority is placed on the dissemination of accurate and timely information through an effective communications network within each college and throughout the system. Personnel involved in transfer issues, such as registrars, admissions officers, counselors, and faculty members, should be encouraged to work together to develop comprehensive ways of addressing problems related to articulation and transfer.

Conclusion

Faculty-based articulation task forces are important vehicles for the identification and resolution of curricular issues in the transferability of liberal arts and science courses in multicampus systems. CUNY's five task forces enabled it to move beyond a unilateral process of course evaluation controlled by the senior colleges to a collaborative process based on mutual respect and cooperation among the colleges. Further, it demonstrates that, aside from the specific recommendations or products that emerge, the process itself has important benefits. In addition to the eighty-five recommendations produced by the task forces, the meetings between faculty led to a gradual erosion of the status-consciousness and elitism that prevails within the senior colleges and to a breaking down of the barriers that preclude effective communication. The feeling of community colleges, expressed by one task force member (Graham, 1987) as being that of "beggars," began to dissolve. Having faculty from each of the seventeen colleges meet face to face and address problems in an open and neutral environment helped to minimize residual arrogance and elitism, however subtle it might be. The task forces also increased the awareness among faculty of the complexities and realities involved in implementing seemingly small changes throughout a university system as large and complex as CUNY.

Thus, systematic activities designed to narrow gaps between policy and practice can lead to improvements in the transferability of credit within multicampus systems where individual units have very diverse missions, goals, and programs. While a balance must be maintained between the legitimate institutional authority of the campuses and the goals of the system at large, addressing issues in a neutral and cooperative environment helps colleges to resolve conflicts in a realistic way. However, such activities must be supported and expanded if the goal of unimpeded access to baccalaureate programs is to be met. Without such support, the external agencies and state legislative bodies concerned with financial exigencies, which have little sensitivity to or understanding of academic and curricular realities, may force compliance. Ultimately, higher education systems that care for their students must speak with the same voice both publicly and privately if they are to carry out their missions of educational mobility and access.

References

Board of Trustees, City University of New York. *Policy on Transfer of CUNY Associate in Arts (A.A.) and Associate in Science (A.S.) Graduates.* New York: Board of Trustees, City University of New York, 1972.

Board of Trustees, City University of New York. *Policy on CUNY Associate in Applied Science (A.A.S.) Graduates.* New York: Board of Trustees, City University of New York, 1973.

Board of Trustees, City University of New York. *Policy on Transfer of Liberal Arts and Science Courses.* New York: Board of Trustees, City University of New York, 1985.

Bowles, D. *CUNY Course Equivalency Guide.* New York: Office of Academic Affairs, City University of New York, 1985.

Florida Department of Education. *Florida Articulation Agreement of 1971.* Tallahassee: Florida Department of Education, 1971.

Graham, S. Comments made at meetings of the City University of New York's Biology Task Force, 1987.

New Jersey Board of Higher Education. *Statewide Plan for Higher Education.* Trenton: New Jersey Board of Higher Education, 1981.

Office of Academic Affairs, City University of New York. *Liberal Arts Degree and Transfers in the City University of New York: An Audit of the 1985 Articulation Policy.* New York: Office of Academic Affairs, City University of New York, 1987a.

Office of Academic Affairs, City University of New York. *Report of the Task Forces in the Liberal Arts and Sciences.* New York: Office of Academic Affairs, City University of New York, 1987b.

Office of the Chancellor, California State Colleges and Universities. *Executive Order 167 on Transfer of Credit.* Los Angeles: Office of the Chancellor, California State Colleges and Universities, 1973.

Office of Institutional Research, City University of New York. *CUNY Data Book, 1984–85.* New York: Office of Institutional Research, City University of New York, 1985.

Richardson, R. C., Jr., and Bender, L. W. *Students in Urban Settings: Achieving the Baccalaureate Degree.* ASHE-ERIC Higher Education Report no. 6. Washington, D.C.: Association for the Study of Higher Education, 1985.

Dympna Bowles is director of articulation in the Office of Academic Affairs at the City University of New York.

Faculty participation within integrated institutional activities is essential for the development of successful transfer articulation agreements.

The Crucial Role of Faculty in Transfer Articulation

Renee Berger, Aida M. Ortiz Ruiz

Transfer has traditionally fallen within the purview of student services, while the task of acquiring articulation agreements has been left to administrators. Excessive paperwork, conventional perspectives, and academic indifference have historically inhibited transfer. Articulation between competing institutions in the same geographical area presents its own set of problems, with competition serving to reinforce many traditional barriers. With all this in mind, Hostos Community College, a unit of the City University of New York (CUNY), conceived of an integrated transfer model developing over three stages, each of which was to involve faculty, student services, and administrative units in complementary ways, with faculty playing the paramount role. Since curriculum is the prerogative of faculty, any question on transfer credit should be theirs to resolve. The fundamental premise of the Hostos articulation model is that, given all the factors that tend to divide two- and four-year faculty within an urban multicultural setting, the one thing they hold in common is their respect for their academic disciplines and commitment to education.

The Setting

Hostos Community College is one unit of a major public urban university that consists of nine senior colleges, seven community colleges,

C. Prager (ed.). *Enhancing Articulation and Transfer.*
New Directions for Community Colleges, no. 61. San Francisco: Jossey-Bass, Spring 1988.

a technical college, a law school, a medical school, and an affiliated school of medicine. Although one would expect to find fewer barriers to transfer articulation within a university system of colleges that have a policy-setting board and urban geography in common, the community colleges within CUNY face the same problems in providing program continuity for their graduates as two-year colleges outside larger urban systems.

In 1973, the CUNY governing board adopted a policy stating that all CUNY community college A.A. and A.S. degree recipients would be accepted as matriculated students at a senior college and that they would be granted a minimum of sixty-four credits toward the baccalaureate degree. More than a decade later, articulation was still being described as a very serious issue. In 1985, the board adopted an additional policy to address the remaining barriers to transfer that mandated the various steps to be taken. This policy is currently in the process of implementation.

Bilingual Education. Hostos serves a predominantly Spanish-speaking, nontraditional population. The college is one of the few in the United States with a comprehensive, transitional Spanish-English bilingual program. The bilingual approach enables the Spanish-dominant student to receive instruction in Spanish and concurrently develop English-language skills to a level of proficiency required for entry into the job market or for transfer to a four-year college. Because it serves an almost entirely minority population, Hostos has become especially attentive to the transfer needs of its students.

Articulation at Hostos. Historically, Hostos had dealt with transfer articulation in a very traditional way. We had a transfer counselor, and we hosted transfer days. Administrative offices concerned themselves with the movement of applications, transcripts, and so forth between the college and receiving institutions. Some articulation took place on a single course-by-course basis, but no formal structure existed for the process, making it largely dependent on sheer chance.

At the same time, experience revealed difficulties, despite a universitywide mandate for the acceptance of credit on transfer. The major unresolved issue was the nature and quality of the acceptance; that is, would credits transfer as electives, as major requirements, or as something else? We learned later, at the first Ford Foundation meeting of the 24 grantees in the Urban Community College Transfer Opportunities Program (UCCTOP), that this question troubled virtually all program participants, regardless of their legal relationships to the four-year colleges.

UCCTOP. The Ford Foundation announced the Urban Community College Transfer Opportunities Program (UCCTOP) in 1983. This new invitational grant program responded to statistical indications that minority student access to higher education took place most frequently through local community colleges, that many students enrolled with the intention of transferring to senior institutions for the bachelor's degree, and that only a small fraction of these students achieved that goal. UCCTOP's stated purpose was to assist selected community colleges in improving their instruction, academic programs, and support services for students transferring to four-year institutions. The Ford Foundation grant enabled Hostos to initiate the transfer articulation model that we had been developing conceptually but that we lacked the resources to implement.

An Integrated Model

The Faculty. Hostos involved faculty in a specific set of articulation-related activities. In general terms, faculty were to determine the exact status of the relationship between Hostos courses and programs and the courses and programs of selected senior colleges and to establish the greatest possible congruence between them. Their charge was to examine, discuss, and negotiate course-by-course equivalence and transferability and examine programs to define problem areas. It was expected that informal discussions with colleagues at senior colleges would clarify or resolve many of these problems, after which faculty were to present internal recommendations on such matters as course requirements and sequences in advance of formal discussions and negotiations bearing on total program articulation agreements. To ensure an informed perspective at this stage, Hostos designed a program of faculty development to support the faculty's broadening awareness of and participation in the articulation process and its curricular implications.

Student Services. The Student Services Division was made responsible for the identification of potential transfer students and for providing follow-up and support to these students throughout their Hostos years and when they transferred to the senior college. This responsibility required student services to develop an identification and follow-up system to be implemented by counselors and a computerized degree requirement checklist (DRC) to assist in student advisement. Student services personnel also developed special transfer seminars to clarify the meaning and career potential of the liberal arts for students and organized a corps of alumni and alumnae advisers from the senior college to assist students who expressed interest in transferring to the institution.

Administrative Support. Administrative support provided an essential underpinning for all the activities. It provided student information and a survey instrument for use by student services. It set up staff contacts and developed procedures to ensure that there would be no institutional obstacles to student transfer and graduation in such areas as admissions and financial aid.

Stage One

Implementation of the integrated institutional approach just described has taken place in three stages. In stage one, the Hostos president established general agreements with four-year colleges on institutional cooperation so that the process could get under way. The president then appointed a faculty audit task force consisting of liberal arts department chairpersons to study and discuss the questions involved in course-by-course articulation and transferability. At about the same time, Hostos started to plan for faculty development.

The Audit Task Force. The first step of the task force was probably the most significant in that it set a particular tone and approach for subsequent activities. The chairpersons, unit coordinators, or both (most departments are composed of several units) reviewed each course in their areas to determine whether a Hostos course had an equivalent at three targeted CUNY senior colleges. They, departmental curriculum committees, or both then listed every course and indicated upper-level equivalents. Thus, it was faculty of the community college who initiated review of its curriculum and deliberations on its articulation.

Task force meetings were characterized by a concern for individual disciplines and by the need for maintaining the integrity of the community college curriculum. Members felt that they had a responsibility to their students, to the college mission, and to the community college concept. The more they read, analyzed, and discussed articulation and transfer issues, the more convinced they became that faculty had to take an active role in articulation.

Faculty Development. Professional development on articulation had to occur so that the faculty could negotiate with their four-year counterparts with informed confidence. We had to create a structure wherein the faculty were knowledgeable about articulation barriers and solutions, an area of expertise that in the past had belonged exclusively to the administration. Once faculty understood and accepted the social and political issues of articulation on the national and local scales, they could proceed to resolve the educational ones. Four-year faculty and two-year faculty had to begin a dialogue, share ideas and concerns, and exchange information. However, internal dialogue had to precede the coordination of intercollege contact and cooperation.

Faculty Development Activities. Faculty development activities have been numerous and continuous. They include a flow of information and articles from the literature to faculty, colloquia with external experts on articulation, and informal meetings. The faculty audit task force used a questionnaire to assess the unit coordinators' perceptions of articulation problems and constraints in specific subject areas. The questionnaire asked respondents to identify particular curriculum area difficulties, state ways in which the area had solved or attempted to solve its articulation problems, describe how articulation had been accomplished (if it had been accomplished), and suggest solutions for general articulation problems. As a result, before two-year faculty met with their four-year colleagues, they were well prepared to show that if the course syllabus is similar, the reading list is comparable, and the teachers have been approved by the same governing board, then there is sufficient evidence to permit transfer and acceptance of credits, courses, and students. Given widespread perceptions of community college instruction among faculty of the senior colleges, this is a very important point.

A Ford Foundation UCCTOP follow-up award supported a series of colloquia for liberal arts and occupational education chairpersons, coordinators, and other interested faculty. These colloquia served to broaden faculty involvement in transfer considerations and to underline the wider context of transfer articulation. The speakers included Dorothy Knoell, postsecondary education administrator of the California Postsecondary Commission, who brought a national perspective to the question, and Ethyle Wolfe, provost of Brooklyn College, who spoke on the core curriculum.

It is obvious that the determination of equivalencies cannot be unilateral. Chief academic officers from senior colleges agreed to assist in the overall articulation project and sent the task force their college catalogues and names of their department chairpersons. Hostos faculty then worked with senior colleagues on a department-by-department and discipline-by-discipline basis to establish equivalencies for each Hostos course, including the exact standing of the Hostos course in relation to senior college distributions or core requirements. The task force compiled the results, and the Hostos dean of faculty distributed them to counterparts at the senior colleges for final determination of equivalencies. The end product was the first official comprehensive equivalency listing for Hostos liberal arts courses, and it had been initiated by community college faculty and developed with input from faculty.

Transfer Questions Raised by Stage One Data. For the first time, Hostos had a clear view of the questions that the search for articulation raises. Some of these questions related to specific courses, but others led inevitably to broader considerations. For example, what can be done when a group of courses at cooperating institutions covers the same total area, but the individual courses that make up this totality appear to be significantly different from school to school? Or, when cooperating institutions adopt distinct core curricula, how does the community college sequence of courses articulate? And, broadest of all, how does articulation occur when the faculties of the respective institutions each maintain that their courses or program designs fulfill the missions of their institutions and maintain the integrity of their curricula?

Student Services and Administrative Support. In the first stage, the main focus for the student services and administrative units was to acquire and computerize student information. Counselors teaching the required freshman orientation course used a special survey to identify potential transfer students.

Faculty Advisement and Use of the DRC. A volunteer faculty liberal arts advisement corps of long standing acquired additional academic advisement and counseling techniques through workshops and discussions and received course transferability information as it developed. The corps also began to use the DRC as a significant advisement tool, since the DRC showed a student's current position in a program—that is, courses taken, courses in progress, and courses to be completed. It also showed the effect of intended or suggested changes in courses and programs on student progress toward graduation. Refinement and updating of the DRC are therefore an ongoing activity.

Alumni and Alumnae Advisement. To cope with the problems of transfer, which can be particularly difficult for minority students, the director of academic advisement added alumni and alumnae advisers to the existing peer advisement program. These advisers have become a very important part of the overall transfer support system. Most of the advisers had already participated in the peer advisement program, and they were all enrolled at four-year colleges. They offer workshops and presentations at Hostos and provide personal encouragement as well as technical information to prospective transferees. In addition, they serve as a friendly contact within the senior college to assist the incoming Hostos transferee in coping with transfer shock.

The Futures Seminar. The Futures Seminar serves as a follow-up to the freshman orientation course. The seven-part course syllabus affords students many opportunities to explore educational options. The program is designed to clarify the meaning of the liberal arts and the solid foundation that the liberal arts provide and to help students discover the many career paths that a liberal arts education can open. Research assignments foster an understanding of the connection between academic majors and careers.

A major objective of the Futures program is to foster the development of transfer skills. Thus the seminar is designed to enhance self-confidence and assertiveness during the transfer process. Students get practice in negotiating acceptance of their academic credits through role playing and other simulations, while the program encourages them to ask questions and persist in moving toward their educational goals.

ESL Students. One section of the seminar particularly addresses students of English as a second language (ESL). It affords maximum opportunity for the reinforcement and practice of English communication skills and includes such activities as visits to senior college campuses and meetings with admissions and recruitment personnel, counselors, and faculty. Initial results of this effort indicate that the seminar—a purely voluntary and noncredit activity—is as successful with ESL students as it is with English-dominant students.

Stage Two

As the course equivalency listings have emerged, the chairpersons have moved to establish transfer tracks by area or discipline based on courses that the faculty audit task force and senior colleges have designated as transferable. In each case, the senior colleges confirm the articulation of the transfer track. As part of the process, Hostos faculty evaluate courses that the senior colleges designate as nontransferable by examining the senior college's syllabi, textbook lists, and final examinations. Their evaluation asks whether faculty quality, reading materials, credits, and hours are comparable.

When the answers are all positive, the Hostos chairperson contacts his or her colleague at the senior college to negotiate course transferability. If there are discrepancies, faculty refer the information to the departmental curriculum committee to decide whether the Hostos course should be changed or whether it is so basic to the mission of the department or college that it should stand.

Stage Three

An additional UCCTOP grant is providing support for the development of joint admissions programs with four-year institutions while efforts to extend the internal integrated articulation transfer support model continue. At this stage, the college is approaching the goal of ensuring junior status for Hostos graduates and of extending the alumni and alumnae adviser system into a joint orientation program with the senior college.

Joint Admissions Program. The aim of the joint admissions program is to provide students with a statement of admission to a four-year articulated program on admission to the community college, pending satisfactory completion of the applicable transfer track curriculum at Hostos.

Program-to-Program Articulation. Hostos is proceeding from course-to-course and discipline-to-discipline articulation to full program-to-program congruence. The one-to-one, colleague-to-colleague relationship between two- and four-year faculties has promoted the organization of Hostos faculty teams established for the development of fully articulated joint programs between the institutions.

The composition and approach of the teams varies with the program area and individuals involved. A department chair and unit coordinator might form a team and make use of their familiarity with the curriculum and ongoing professional activities at senior colleges to discuss emerging problems with senior college staff, or a department chairperson might pave the way for an experienced faculty member to conduct an in-depth program review relative to the offerings of senior colleges. Again, when difficulties arise over the content of occupational or preprofessional programs, the team might need to involve basic skills chairs or coordinators, or a team might need to involve the president in order to make the first contacts with the senior college.

All teams work independently within established guidelines. They report to the director of academic activities and, when completing agreements or reaching deadlocks, to the dean of faculty. At this stage, all efforts lead back to the senior administrative level in order to reach successful closure.

Stage Three Faculty Development. At the stage of seeking to ensure fully articulated curricula and joint admissions, the teams require development that focuses on still broader aspects of articulation. Hostos is developing workshops to be conducted by external experts in such areas as the role in articulation of community college occupational and liberal arts faculty; writing across the curriculum, with a focus on discipline discourse and faculty networking; and enhancement of the critical thinking skills required for academic success in content courses.

Stage Three Alumni and Alumnae Advisement. Student services has moved to establish a more formal structure for the corps of alumni and alumnae advisers, using institutional data and faculty members who maintain contact with graduates to identify those attending the CUNY senior colleges. Advisers are selected after a review of academic records and interviews. They attend a formal training program that takes place throughout the academic year. A series of workshops instructs them on college and university policies and procedures related to transfer, use of the CUNY articulation guide, and ways of working with students. Several training sessions focus on counseling skills that advisers need in order to help students make decisions about transfer, provide them with assistance in the actual process, and offer them support after they enroll at the four-year college.

Each adviser spends several hours each week in the Hostos peer adviser office assisting prospective transfer students to make choices regarding their continued study and to help effect the transfer process. Advisers also hold workshops, informal gatherings, and panels with question-and-answer periods.

Summer Orientation. Hostos holds orientation sessions during the summer before transfer, geared specifically to each receiving institution. An adviser who is a student at the institution conducts the session and offers information on evaluation of credits, placement tests, administrative offices, counseling, and financial aid, as well as tips on where to go with various problems. We expect one outcome to be a bond between the student and the adviser, who can offer continued support on the four-year college campus. Student services is looking to expand the role of the advisers by developing and implementing an orientation program for graduating transfers on the senior college campus collaboratively with the senior colleges.

Summary

As a result of the multistage approach to articulation and transfer just described, which involves faculty at all stages, Hostos has been able to reduce the problem of articulation from a general to a well-defined one in specific areas of individual programs. Much of our future effort will be directed toward improvements and refinements. These efforts will include redesigning the DRC to reflect the different sequences for joint admissions students and establishing procedures both for the accurate reporting of statistics on transfer students by senior institutions and for following up on these students to graduation.

Renee Berger is director of grants and contracts and project director of the Hostos UCCTOP project.

Aida M. Ortiz Ruiz teaches English and directs the academic articulation activities initiated by the UCCTOP project.

Transfer relationships are easier for two- and four-year technological programs to achieve than they are for most other programs in that the curriculum is highly structured. At the same time, they are harder to achieve in that the upper-division courses depend much more directly on the lower-division courses taught at the community college.

Transfer Relationships Between Two-Year and Four-Year Technological Programs

Gary Thomas

Technicians and engineers represent one of the largest groups of professionals in the United States. For example, engineers are second in number only to elementary and secondary teachers. Technicians can develop their skills on the job or through specialized education programs, many of which are offered by community and junior colleges. Engineers may come from the ranks of high school graduates who go directly to college or from the ranks of technicians in industry who acquire further education at colleges and universities. Ideally, the preparation that technicians receive should enable them to pursue additional formal education later in life that leads to new professional opportunities.

The fact that engineers enter the profession at multiple levels means that articulation relationships between two- and four-year colleges would be vital even if four-year colleges were not concerned with the drop in the number of high school graduates. Now, the drop in college enrollments may help some baccalaureate degree-granting institutions that have overlooked their responsibility for articulation in the past to

C. Prager (ed.). *Enhancing Articulation and Transfer.*
New Directions for Community Colleges, no. 61. San Francisco: Jossey-Bass, Spring 1988.

see the need for it more clearly. In any case, the preparation of community college students for study at four-year colleges of engineering makes it important for smooth articulation relationships to exist.

To facilitate transfer, the New Jersey Institute of Technology (NJIT) has worked with community colleges in developing four variants on articulation that go beyond the traditional A.A. or A.S. degree transfer arrangement: 2+2 programs, cooperative education programs, consortial arrangements, and dual admissions. Each variant involves the identification and selection of students well before their junior year. Some of these programs were initiated by NJIT, others by community colleges. While engineering provides the context for this chapter, the articulation designs discussed here can serve as models for other disciplines.

Engineering Program Articulation

Some states require senior colleges and universities to accept all students who graduate from an accredited community college. At the same time, most baccalaureate-accrediting agencies require the institution granting the four-year degree to take overall responsibility for the integrity of the degree, whether all the courses taken toward the degree were taken at the baccalaureate institution or not. As a result, even if community college graduates are accepted automatically, they may need to repeat many courses if the courses taken at the two-year college do not fit the requirements of the curriculum at the four-year college.

Further, if the level and subject matter covered in comparable courses are not truly comparable, students may not in fact be prepared for advanced courses. This is especially true of mathematics and science preparation for engineering curricula, since most of the professional courses are taken at the upper-division level. The fact that these observations state the obvious does not mean that their implications can be evaded or overlooked in the transfer relationship between two- and four-year colleges.

Pyramidal Nature of Science and Technology Curricula. Engineering subjects, like those in science and mathematics, are pyramidal. This fact is made manifest when students do not have the mathematical maturity and skills to complete engineering courses satisfactorily. The pyramidal nature of the curriculum requires ongoing discussion between the faculties of the two- and four-year schools who prepare students for graduation from the four-year college. Without interinstitutional dialogue, neither institution can develop sufficient confidence in the other to make the needed modifications in its curricula and advisement systems to ensure that students have a reasonable chance of success.

Providing a Data Base. In New Jersey, no mandatory transfer agreements exist between the state-supported universities and the community colleges. Despite this, NJIT has established curriculum-by-curriculum articulation agreements with nearly all state community colleges. These agreements call for semiannual meetings to discuss the progress of transfer students at NJIT. Table 1 is typical of the data that NJIT provides to the community colleges to chart their graduates' progress.

Table 1 indicates the overall performance of students in several programs. The first column shows the cumulative grade point average (GPA) of all community college transfers in 1985 by college. The second column represents the cumulative grade point average earned by these students at NJIT in their first year. The third column is the ratio of the cumulative grade point average at the community college to the cumulative GPA earned at NJIT. The last column represents the number of transfer students from each community college that year.

As Table 1 suggests, the disparity between the performance of transfer students at the community college and at NJIT is wider for students from some community colleges than it is for students from others. In addition to global data, NJIT provides the sending colleges with data related to individual student performance that includes the student's cumulative GPA, transfer credits, transfer GPA, and term GPA. Such data can provide a basis of further discussion about the probable causes for comparative success rates and lead to program modifications where needed.

The aggregate and individual student data supply the basis of the semiannual dialogue between the faculties of the two institutions. It

Table 1. Grades Earned by Transferring Students

Community College	*Grade Point Average at Community College*	*Grade Point Average at NJIT*	*Ratio*	*Number*
A	3.11	3.06	0.98	12
B	3.04	2.90	0.95	14
C	2.80	2.73	0.98	52
D	2.78	2.68	0.96	55
E	2.94	2.66	0.90	11
F	2.90	2.59	0.89	12
G	3.23	2.53	0.78	26
H	3.00	2.50	0.83	16
I	2.83	2.38	0.84	43
J	3.03	2.26	0.75	11
K	2.99	2.15	0.72	79
Average	2.96	2.51	0.85	331

might be expected that such dialogue would be difficult to sustain. However, from the perspective of a university-level chief academic officer, it is no more difficult to sustain than the discussion that must take place between faculties within the same institution where it is typical for departments of mathematics and science and engineering to answer to separate deans and to have their own measures of professional success.

2+2 Engineering Technology Programs

New Jersey was relatively late in its creation of a community college system. The first community college opened in 1966. Prior to that time, part of the state's need for industrial technicians was satisfied by NJIT's certificate program. As the community college system grew, NJIT's role in technical education steadily declined. Its major engineering technology emphasis has since shifted to the baccalaureate degree. Because the engineering technology baccalaureate program was created as a senior-level curriculum, the faculties of NJIT and the community colleges have worked closely since the inception of the program to ensure compatibility between the upper-division courses taught at NJIT and the lower-division courses taught at the community colleges. This articulation effort is not without intrinsic difficulties, given the fact that the community colleges have to educate the majority of their technology students both for immediate employment on graduation and for the possibility of eventual transfer.

General Education Conflict. Two events in 1985 required alterations in the curriculum. The first was passage of revised community college general education requirements by the state board of higher education. These requirements mandated certain courses at the two-year level ordinarily found at NJIT in the third or fourth year. The second was NJIT's desire to apply its own new general university requirements to all programs at the institution, including engineering technology. Both reforms responded to the general opinion that a college degree should provide students with skills and knowledge that can only be imparted by higher education.

Accreditation Conflict. At the same time, NJIT was undergoing review by the Technology Accreditation Board of the Accreditation Board for Engineering and Technology (ABET). ABET made it quite clear that NJIT was responsible for all four years of its education program in technology even if it offered only the last two years of the program.

Resolution. Because of the avenues of communication that had developed between NJIT and the community colleges over the years, it was possible to resolve these conflicts by meeting with the community colleges as a group and as individual institutions. Meetings between the faculties of the respective schools formalized mutually agreed upon course-by-course equivalencies for all articulated programs, including the technology program, and individual articulation agreements were modified to accommodate the general education requirements imposed by the state on the community colleges.

Need for Early Transfer Counseling. The responsibility that ABET places on the senior institution provides another reason for beginning the transfer process early in a student's two-year course of study. Ideally, this process should start as soon as the student has selected courses that are prerequisite to courses in the upper division. What is indicated here goes far beyond advisement. It requires direct involvement with the institution to which the student plans to transfer. This principle applies to regular transfer and articulated 2+2 programs, as well as to the more unusual patterns involving cooperative education, dual admissions, and consortial programs discussed in the following sections.

Cooperative Education

One of the most common types of engineering cooperative education program is an alternating work study program during the third-year course sequence. To have maximum effect, the coop student must be placed into a job that takes advantage of the education that he or she received during the first two years. It is typical for such students to be paired on the job; that is, two students with approximately the same background and level of skills are identified for one employer to fill one position on an alternating schedule. The school that arranges the placement must know the students' educational backgrounds in detail, as well as their educational and professional plans for when they complete their studies.

In order for community college students to have an equal chance of participating in a coop program with students who start as freshmen at the senior college, the community college students must be interviewed while they are still in their second year. Further, their preparation must be equivalent to that of the students who begin their college career at the senior college.

NJIT recently began planning for the implementation of a cooperative education program that will place students from community colleges before they take their first class at NJIT. Prospective engineering technology students will be the first to take part. In the past, no engineering technology student has been eligible for the coop program because of the curriculum's 2+2 nature and because of the requirement for completion of NJIT credit before placement in a work experience.

A Consortial Approach to Articulation: Computer-Integrated Manufacturing (CIM)

In 1984, NJIT began a computer-integrated manufacturing (CIM) program to address the progressive decline in the production of goods within the United States during the last decade. The program used technological advances that permit computer-aided and -integrated machine design and product manufacturing. The equipment necessary to prepare students to take part in the dramatic changes that the introduction of this technology will cause is very expensive. Instruction requires a specialized faculty of professionals who are difficult to attract to university teaching. The state of New Jersey agreed to provide NJIT with the resources necessary to introduce advanced manufacturing into its curriculum if it worked out ways of providing community colleges with ways of participating.

The agreement to develop regional CIM consortia of NJIT and the community colleges led to the decision that a factory of the future would be created at NJIT and that community college faculty would have access to the factory in order to teach project and design courses if such courses could not be taught on their own campuses. When the community college does not have faculty with the specializations needed for these courses, NJIT supplies the instruction for the first two-year CIM-related components of the curriculum.

The development of the CIM consortium is more than another version of the 2+2 articulation format, since it involves a four-year curriculum designed with the input of two- and four-year faculty and supported by faculty and equipment shared by both educational levels. The model has great potential for local, regional, and state program development, since community colleges and senior institutions can profit from the sharing of specialized faculty and costly equipment.

Dual Admissions

In the overlapping programs so far discussed—2+2, cooperative education, and the consortium—it is very important to know in advance how students are likely to perform in the upper division. Curricula close enough to foster confidence that transfer students, even those at the lower levels of academic performance, have a reasonable chance of graduating from the senior institution make dual admissions programs possible. Dual admissions programs enlarge the transfer options available to community college students.

As of the 1986–1987 academic year, high school students with a certain level of preparation or an adequate level of performance in preparatory courses are offered joint admission to a community college and NJIT. Admission to NJIT is contingent on completion of the lower division of the program at the community college.

Dual admissions benefits the community college by attracting students who otherwise might go directly to a four-year college. NJIT benefits from the transfers to it of students who have a high probability of completing its programs but whose high school records are too weak to enable them to be admitted directly as freshmen. It benefits students by allowing them to know in advance that they will be accepted into a baccalaureate program and to attend college for the first two years locally, which helps to reduce the total cost of their four years of higher education. It benefits the state by reducing the total cost of state support to education through the baccalaureate, since the state's contribution to the support of community college education is usually substantially less than its contribution to the support of other state-supported colleges.

Conclusions

Clearly, transfer arrangements make sense for all concerned: The student who may not have taken high school seriously gets another chance at four years of higher education, the state is able to provide students with opportunities to receive high-quality college education at a reduced total cost, and the colleges are able to differentiate their missions without closing their doors to students who would otherwise be excluded from universities for financial reasons or for deficiencies in preparation. However, at least in the case of the technological professions, the special restrictions of the senior colleges should be kept in mind in developing transfer arrangements: First, accreditation is beneficial to most curricula. However, accreditation reviews can cause senior colleges to change their curricula abruptly and in ways that can appear arbitrary to community colleges. Second, most accrediting agencies require senior institutions to assume responsibility for the entire curriculum that the student follows, whether or not the student takes all the courses at the same institution. Third, since success in technological education depends in large measure on the material normally covered in the lower division, senior institutions will have a legitimate concern for the details of what is taught in individual courses.

There are many reasons why students may wish to attend a four-year institution directly out of high school. However, there are growing numbers of students who do not. For these students, especially for students in the technologies, it is important to provide transfer opportunities that offer high-quality education with natural breaks that allow for the possibility of career reorientation.

Gary Thomas is vice-president for academic affairs at New Jersey Institute of Technology.

Despite charges that accreditation policies penalize the community college transfer student, community colleges can negotiate successful articulation agreements for their business programs if they use comprehensive articulation models applicable to other disciplines as well.

Accreditation and Articulation of Business Programs

Mary Robertson-Smith

In American postsecondary education, two types of voluntary accrediting activity have evolved: regional activity and specialized or programmatic activity. While regional accreditation focuses on the entire institution, specialized accreditation focuses on specific programs or parts of the institution. The agencies involved in this type of accrediting activity are national in scope. The primary purview of their evaluation is judgment that programs do or do not meet standards of good practice in the field. Dickey and Miller (1972) note that such agencies represent the interests both of practitioners and of educators by promoting established standards and aiding programs to maintain those standards.

The purpose of specialized accreditation is to help to maintain program quality. By setting standards to which disciplinary representatives have mutually agreed, specialized accreditation has generally helped individual disciplines to respond to changing technologies and knowledge bases. Most of the agencies involved in the regional and specialized accreditation process have assisted two-to-four-year program articulation efforts by focusing on planning for quality programs and by placing the emphasis on accountability and evaluation.

However, one such agency, the American Assembly of Collegiate Schools of Business (AACSB), has been criticized for accreditation stan-

C. Prager (ed.). *Enhancing Articulation and Transfer.*
New Directions for Community Colleges, no. 61. San Francisco: Jossey-Bass, Spring 1988.

dards that impede rather than help to effectuate smooth transfer of credit from two- to four-year programs. The critics maintain that the AACSB violates the principle of collegial review and agreement, since it excludes the two-year sector from membership and since its accreditation guidelines hinder effective articulation from two-year programs. This chapter explores the reasons for community college discontent with the AACSB position, the movement to seek redress inside and outside the AACSB, and some approaches that individual colleges can use in the interim to effectuate successful articulation agreements for their business programs.

Bases of Community College Concern

Savage (1986, pp. 1, 3) summed up the grounds for community college concern about the AACSB position in these terms: "Because the American Assembly of Collegiate Schools of Business (AACSB) sets accreditation standards specifying that undergraduate business programs should concentrate their professional courses in the last 2 years of a 4-year program, and should offer only a limited amount of work below the junior year, community college transfer students typically lose a year or more of college work when they decide to pursue a baccalaureate degree in an accredited AACSB program. . . . Compounding the problem is the preponderance of adult students attending community colleges, who 'back into' higher education, taking a few business courses to enhance their job skills, move on to an associate degree, and then decide to pursue a baccalaureate degree. Unfortunately, virtually none of their technical credits will transfer and they must retake the same courses to earn the bachelor's degree." Four years earlier, Bonnell (1982) had declared the situation to be at an "impasse" and called for legislative or judicial intervention into what he saw as the AACSB's prescriptive application of its prerogatives.

The complaints have centered on what seems to be a double standard. The AACSB guidelines permit several methods for validation of credit from the two-year college, including proficiency examinations or successful passage of advanced courses taken at the senior institution. Under AASCB guidelines, validation tests that may be administered to two-year college students in junior standing are not required of four-year native juniors. Transferees are often tested on work that they completed several semesters before. Moreover, standards do not seem to be comparable, since they prohibit transferees but not native juniors from receiving credits for lower-level courses taken at the four-year college if they do not pass their upper-level course work.

However, the major complaint seems to be that the AACSB position is incompatible with community college education. Indeed, critics have noted the apparent disparity between the stated goal of the AACSB's major committee, which is called Equal Opportunity for Minorities, and the seemingly unequal treatment accorded to two-year college students, many of whom are minorities seeking to enter AACSB-accredited institutions from community college programs. As Blanchard (1986) argued in his response to a Massachusetts Board of Regents requirement that public sector institutions seek accreditation from the AACSB, such a requirement suggests a deep misunderstanding of the role of community colleges in open-access education, as well as of common patterns of course enrollment among community college students.

A national confrontation may be brewing. The federal Division of Eligibility and Agency Evaluation (DEAE) acknowledged community college concerns in 1980 and granted a two-year (rather than a typical four-year) renewal to the AACSB as a recognized accreditation body. However, in 1983, the AACSB was granted the normal four-year renewal in the absence of any third-party input. The AACSB approached the DEAE again in 1987. It is anticipated that this will become a major forum for the expression of community college concern with the AACSB position, unless the organization makes changes from within.

Articulation Possibilities Within the AACSB Framework

Is it possible to establish successful articulation of business programs within the AACSB framework? The answer is a somewhat qualified yes. From the AACSB standpoint, several colleges have good business program articulation arrangements. In a personal communication (telephone interview, April 27, 1987) Milton Blood of the agency staff cited the following: Canisius College in Buffalo, New York; Florida International University in Miami; the University of Alabama at Birmingham; the University of Tennessee at Chattanooga; Eastern Washington University in Cheney; and Western Michigan University in Kalamazoo.

According to Dr. Blood, the articulation agreements of these and similar AACSB-accredited programs have four characteristics: First, written agreements and materials are readily available to all students in the program, so that community college students are aware of all expectations for transfer. Second, detailed discussion of the programs has taken place between the two schools, and the discussion has included validation methodology. Third, discussion of the programs has involved faculty and administrators. Fourth, several validation methods, including American College Testing Program tests, are generally available. On the issue of validation, Blood stated, "The method of validation is not the key issue if the institutions are really trying to make the process work. The method becomes key when one institution does not want to make it work. What the institutions use as a validation fades as an issue as long as somewhere in the institution a file shows how the validation has occurred and that there was not just automatic transfer of credits. The files must show that the institutions are in charge of the quality of education and that they are managing the process" (Blood, 1987).

Articulation at the Local Level. Gordan (1975) discussed the AACSB validation process in a speech to the American Accounting Association. He concluded that the most effective resolution of the transfer problem occurs at the local level, where two-year colleges can meet with representatives of the baccalaureate degree-granting institutions to which their students transfer.

Local resolution has worked fairly well in New Jersey, where college-to-college negotiation of direct agreements seems to have become the primary method of addressing AACSB standards for community college course validation. Typically, this negotiation results in articulation agreements based on course-by-course evaluation, program evaluation, and review of evaluation materials generated by outside consultants. The agreements that have been developed for business programs involve a systematic process that establishes articulation program goals, development of activities by the two- and the four-year college to meet these goals, development of outcome measures, and planning for the use of results by both parties. The scope and sequence of course content and outcome studies of transfer students' performance in advanced courses are important components of the course and program articulation approach. Such institutions as Rutgers University and the New Jersey Institute of Technology regularly send to community colleges the grades and other survival indicators of transfer students in business and other curricula. In each case, the receiving institution has developed an approach with the sending institution that focuses on mutual improvement of the instructional process.

Montclair and William Patterson State Colleges used a two-stage approach to develop their articulation efforts, first defining a model for the articulation of general education course components for two-year programs, then defining programmatic articulation for individual programs, such as business and accounting. Rutgers has based its articulation efforts on a course-by-course assessment. In either model, the junior and senior institutions understand that the process will enhance the instructional program at both levels by providing valuable feedback and statistical profiles that can be used for evaluation of the curriculum.

New Jersey has developed a systematic program of basic skills testing, remediation, and posttesting based on a common statewide examination. In this sense, there is a common ground for placement of students in business and accounting courses at every institution. In addition, state regulation in New Jersey has established standards for the distribution of general education components for two- and four-year colleges that are roughly equivalent. It is anticipated that a program of outcomes to evaluate critical thinking and higher-order cognitive skills of students at the end of two years of higher education will be in place by 1988. All these measures may be contributing factors to the development of effective articulation and validation for two-year-college business programs.

The Process of Negotiation. Although these contributing factors may be favorable, the actual negotiation of articulation arrangements requires a carefully structured process. For example, Bergen Community College in Paramus has succeeded in developing articulation agreements with sixteen in-state and fifteen out-of-state schools. It has found that if articulation efforts are to succeed, the top leaders at both institutions must be committed to the process. For this reason, it is usually helpful for the presidents of the community college and the senior college to meet as the initial step. At this meeting, they set the tone for subsequent discussions and establish their institution's commitment to the process. At this meeting, a review of statistics related to the number of students interested in transferring to the senior college has been found helpful in establishing the desirability of effective articulation. The data should be very specific and include such elements as the grade point averages of students who have transferred credits from the two-year college, the number of community college alumni who have graduated from the four-year school, the potential "market" among future graduates from two-year programs, and most important, the ratio of credits earned at the community college to credits accepted by the upper-level program. These analyses will enable the institutions to develop a strategic plan for articulation involving the deans and faculty, who then meet to develop the actual articulation plan.

In order to establish actual program comparability or the need for one or both of the institutions to develop program comparability, the meetings involving faculty and deans should deal with program specifics, including program goals at the respective institutions, outcome assessments of these goals, individual course requirements, and outcome measures for each course. In addition to the specifics of community college and senior college programs, the articulation document should address general principles, such as notification of changes in the curriculum at either institution, catalogue requirements, policies regarding the transfer of D grades, and the process for revision or termination of the agreement. The document should include the four-year curriculum sequence and identify the portion of the curriculum that takes place at each institution.

Bergen's experience suggests that if two-year institutions approach the process of AACSB validation not in a spirit of confrontation but from the perspective of program improvement, effective articulation can develop. In a sense, this approach to validation of business programs resembles the successful self-study process, which has the attributes identified by Kells (1980): The process is internally motivated, top leadership is committed to the process, the design is appropriate to the circumstances, and the process makes an informed attempt to clarify organizational goals and assess achievement of the goals for purposes of improvement.

The Future of Business Program Accreditation and Articulation

Community colleges continue to press for participation at the national level in efforts to establish accreditation guidelines for business programs. Although several other specialized accreditation agencies, including the Accreditation Board for Engineering and Technology and the National League of Nursing, accredit two-year and four-year programs in separate processes, the AACSB has yet to include two-year colleges in its membership. Currently, it has approximately 800 members, including four-year programs, nonaccredited schools, business firms, and government and professional organizations—but not two-year colleges. According to agency officials, proposals for AACSB accreditation of two-year programs are still in the talking stages.

Membership status and two-year program accreditation should improve communication between sending institutions and AACSB colleges. Until these things take place, the AACSB has developed validation techniques that can be viewed either as a unique opportunity to promote curriculum evaluation and articulation or as an irritating obstacle to effective transfer for community college business students.

References

Blanchard, B. "A Response to Recent Board of Regents Action on Business Administration Education and a Critique of the Call for Business Administration Accreditation." Paper presented to the Board of Regents of Higher Education in Massachusetts, 1986. 13 pp. (ED 271 161)

Bonnell, A. T. "Prescriptive Specialized Accreditation: Implication for Urban Community Colleges." In F. C. Kintzer (ed.), *Improving Articulation and Transfer Relationships.* New Directions for Community Colleges, no. 39. San Francisco: Jossey-Bass, 1982.

Dickey, F. G., and Miller, J. W. *A Current Perspective on Accreditation.* Report no. 7. Washington, D.C.: ERIC Clearinghouse on Higher Education, 1972. 73 pp. (ED 068 071)

Gordan, D. "The Transfer Credit Problem: Can Accountants Add 2+2?" Speech presented at the American Accounting Association meeting, Anaheim, Calif., Dec. 7, 1975. 12 pp. (ED 119 801)

Kells, H. R. *Self-Study Process: A Guide for Postsecondary Institutions.* Washington, D.C.: American Council on Education, 1980.

Savage, D. D. "Two-Year Colleges and the AACSB." Unpublished paper, July 1986. 9 pp. (ED 272 224)

Mary Robertson-Smith is vice-president and dean of instruction at Bergen Community College in Paramus, New Jersey.

Transfer agreements in allied health can be successfully negotiated by using competency-based education as the theoretical framework.

Winning Together: Negotiating Transfer Agreements in Allied Health

Elizabeth C. King

Nichole S. has graduated from the state university with an associate degree as a medical laboratory technician (MLT). Her career goal is to complete a bachelor's degree in medical technology. She makes an appointment to meet with the program director at the same state university, since the school offers both the two- and the four-year degree in the field. To her dismay, she learns that she will be able to transfer her general education courses but not her MLT courses. "But some of the same faculty teach in both programs," she responds in disbelief. "Oh, but those MLT courses were all taught at a different level. Didn't you know that MLTs are not taught any problem-solving skills?" Nichole leaves feeling alienated from her first alma mater. In all probability, she will never return to that campus or contribute to its fund-raising drives. Six months later, she transfers to a comprehensive state university that will accept a significant portion of her MLT coursework.

James W. is an experienced radiological technologist who received his initial professional preparation at a hospital. He has two years of work experience in a large tertiary-care center, and he has received on-the-job training in ultrasound. His goal is to complete an associate

C. Prager (ed.). *Enhancing Articulation and Transfer.*
New Directions for Community Colleges, no. 61. San Francisco: Jossey-Bass, Spring 1988.

degree in radiological technology. At his interview with the community college program director, he is told that the college does not recognize hospital-based training. The program director explains, "We must maintain our standards, you know." "But I hold state licensure, and I have been a competent practitioner for two years. I was trained in a hospital setting with state-of-the-art technology and equipment," James replies.

Change the names, and the two cases just described can be found in endless variants. The examples help to illustrate why the Kentucky Council on Higher Education, a state coordinating board, decided to foster the development of a comprehensive statewide articulated system for allied health education that encompassed all postsecondary allied health programs, whether college, postsecondary vocational, proprietary, or hospital based.

What Did We Accomplish?

Ultimately, approximately thirty transfer agreements were negotiated. Competency-based education was used as the theoretical developmental and negotiating framework. These agreements were part of the Kentucky Allied Health Project, the first effort in the nation to design a statewide system for allied health education coordinating all levels of allied health programs in all types of educational institutions. Approximately 100 faculty, clinicians, and administrators from clinical laboratory sciences, dental auxiliaries, nutrition and dietetics, radiological sciences, rehabilitation therapies, and respiratory therapy worked together to design models permitting a transition from one education level to another with a minimum loss of time and academic credit.

How Did We Do It?

How did we take a state with a variety of allied health preparation levels and delivery systems and develop transfer agreements that provide a flexible system of education and eliminate artificially imposed barriers? This section describes the setting for the project and the process used and makes suggestions for those who would like to adapt our model to their unique needs.

Setting. The Kentucky Allied Health Project (KAHP) was the result of a process that began in 1972 when the Kentucky Revised Statutes strengthened the ability of the Council on Higher Education to act as a planning and coordinating body for public higher education. A Health Sciences Advisory Committee created in 1972 was charged with developing recommendations for the future needs of allied health education. The committee appointed a task force that in turn established ad hoc disciplinary study groups in five major health discipline categories. A year of monthly meetings and discussion resulted in a report (Kentucky Council on Higher Education, 1975) that identified twelve allied health education issues in Kentucky and made recommendations for their resolution. The report noted that the limited articulation and coordination among and between allied health and health-related education programs compromised the extent to which these programs met Kentucky's health manpower and service needs.

Organization. With the help of a grant from the United States Department of Health and Human Services, the Kentucky Council on Higher Education set about to develop a statewide articulated allied health educational system (Kirchner, 1978) in six phases. This chapter discusses the first four phases.

Phase 1: Planning

After a review of the literature and a synthesis of the available data, KAHP compiled a complete directory of all state allied health programs. This inventory provided the basis for activating the discipline advisory groups in phase 2.

The fifteen-member Allied Health Task Force was composed of representatives from the public colleges and universities, independent colleges and universities, and vocational schools; practicing clinicians; and hospitals. The baccalaureate degree-granting institutions were represented by the deans of the units responsible for allied health; the community colleges, by the system's assistant vice-president; the vocational education system, by the unit director of health and personnel services; and the hospitals, by a hospital administrator—in other words, individuals with considerable line responsibility for the quality, delivery, and evaluation of allied health programs. The task force was the major governing body of the articulation project. It provided general coordination, helped to secure support from essential publics, and provided guidance for the six disciplinary advisory groups, which were the actual working groups for the development of transfer agreements. The guidance that the task force provided to the six discipline advisory groups was critical to the success of the project, because it provided strong administrative support to what were essentially faculty groups.

Phase 2: Comparing Curricula

The task force recommended about fifteen individuals for each group. The number was large, but it was required in order to provide a balanced representation from all the sectors. The central concept behind the selection of members was that those responsible for implementing project recommendations should assume key leadership positions in developing the recommendations and that responsibility should be shared between educational institutions and the statewide coordinating board for planning.

The advisory groups began by holding monthly meetings. Each meeting was held at a different institution. The host institution provided a tour of its facilities. Wonderful things happened as a result of these visits. For example, many senior faculty had not seen the community colleges' laboratory facilities—and they were impressed. The camaraderie and the mutual respect that developed as a result of these visits helped the respective faculties during actual transfer negotiations. After every participant institution had hosted a meeting, it was agreed that future meetings would be held at a central location in order to minimize travel.

Competency-based education is an ideal theoretical framework for the development of allied health articulation because it provides a statement of the roles and responsibilities for which the student is being prepared; objectives explicitly stating the skills, knowledge, and attitudes expected of program graduates; an instructional program congruent with the expected outcomes; and a program monitored, evaluated, and changed as a result of evaluation. Allied health education has had a long competency-based history. Curricula are designed to prepare learners to function in roles defined in terms of behaviors expected in the job setting (May, 1979). This historic emphasis on competency-based education precedes the current emphasis on outcomes assessment and value added, deeply rooted as it is in the need to prepare clinical practitioners for safe practice.

Next, the task force developed a curricular component form to gather systematic information about the competency-based components of individual programs. The form asked for all preprofessional and professional courses required in the curriculum; course clock hours, credit hours, percent of lecture and laboratory teaching, minimal grade or competency level accepted, flexibility of course sequencing; and types of clinical affiliations used (for example, gentleman's agreement business letter, memorandum of agreement, or actual contract). The form also collected information about the percent of students' total clinical experience, the number and status of clinical instructors, the use of learning objectives, and the method and timing of the students' clinical evaluation.

The most critical components of these data were the course descriptions, outlines, statements of competency-based objectives, and methods of evaluation for each course in the curriculum. These data made it possible to compare programs substantiating concepts presented in an integrated manner as students were acquiring necessary hands-on skills.

It was assumed that programs aimed at educating individuals to practice in the same discipline at different levels taught similar skills and knowledge. Working from this assumption and from pertinent curriculum information, the discipline advisory groups identified the program similarities, that is, the transferable competencies. Where courses were not taught with instructional objectives based on essential competencies geared to safe practice, transferable competencies could not be identified, and transfer negotiations were not achieved.

Phase 3: Articulation Review

The discipline advisory groups and the Allied Health Task Force met about three times a year to review developed curricula, review the articulation designs within each discipline, discuss recommendations for implementing and finalizing draft articulation agreements, and discuss recommendations for implementing, monitoring, and evaluating the system.

These meetings gave the groups an opportunity not only to share their results but also to discuss broader and less measurable outcomes of the process. Among these outcomes was the perception among project participants that one of the most important project outcomes lay in the emergence of mutual respect between and among faculty from the several sectors. This respect enhanced communication and led to curriculum change by those who came to see themselves not as second-class citizens in higher education but as partners or coequals within a system.

Phase 4: Developing and Negotiating Transfer Agreements

Two types of transfer agreements emerged, block and course, in both systemwide and program- or institution-specific formats.

Block Transfer Agreements. The block transfer agreement awarded a specific number of credit hours for completion of an education sequence. It was most useful in considerations bearing on the award of credit from hospital-based or vocational education programs. For example, the University of Louisville's radiological technology program awarded forty-five credits for completion of the Good Samaritan Hospital's radiological technology certificate program. This block transfer agreement addressed the problem that James W. had experienced. Similarly, a block transfer agreement was arrived at between the vocational education programs for respiratory therapy technicians and the associate degree programs for respiratory therapists.

Most educators are comfortable with course transfer but less comfortable with block transfer. However, block transfer of credit is a logical solution to the problem posed by parallelism between certain hospital-based or postsecondary vocational education instruction and training and the instruction and training provided by collegiate programs. While such programs are not planned on a credit hour basis, they are competency based for allied health, and they can be validated by such external criteria as student success on licensing, registration, or other certification examinations.

Course-Specific Transfer Agreements. The course-specific transfer agreement was most useful for the award of credit from an associate to a bachelor's degree program. Nichole's problem—transferring credits from a medical laboratory technician program—was solved by a course-specific transfer agreement.

Systemwide Agreements. In Kentucky, the community colleges are organized as a system under a single administrative unit. As a result, the curriculum for all similar programs is the same. Consequently, a transfer agreement negotiated for one community college program applies to all other community college programs. The same is true for the postsecondary vocational education system. In the end, five allied health programs were included in one systemwide agreement.

Program- and Institution-Specific Agreements. Each program- or institution-specific agreement is limited to specific programs or institutions. The agreements reached for the physical therapist assistant program at Jefferson Community College and for the physical therapy program at the University of Louisville typify this type of agreement.

Career Mobility Models. Within the block and course transfer formats, four career mobility transfer models emerged.

The preprofessional curriculum model provides for the completion of general education requirements and prerequisites for the professional curriculum. The latter are offered on an upper-division basis and lead to the baccalaureate. This is the typical route for occupational therapy, physical therapy, and medical technology. Credit transfer problems are minimal.

The basic professional curricula are typically taught by two-year colleges granting the associate in applied science degree. These courses prepare graduates for the necessary licensure or external examinations leading to professional status in such disciplines as dental hygiene, radiological technology, and respiratory therapy. Few upper-level articulated program options are available to students in these programs who wish to further their higher education. Thus, these students often seek out unarticulated baccalaureate programs leading to teaching certification, administrative preparation, or basic science degrees. Transferring credit from basic professional curricula requires the senior institution to evaluate the transfer merit of programs that differ from the traditional associate degree transfer programs. Many of the difficulties inherent in transfer could be surmounted by consideration of block credit.

In the intermediate professional curricula, the completed course of study leads to an intermediate level of professional certification within a discipline, such as certified occupational therapy assistant or medical laboratory technician. Transferring to an upper-division program has been historically difficult because the two-year and four-year program sequences are incompatible. The traditional route to advanced professional study has thus tended to be a preprofessional curriculum for two-year students who intend from the outset to get the four-year degree, and loss of transfer credit for students who first seek intermediate professional certification through two-year programs.

Removal of Articulation Barriers

At first blush, the development of transfer sequences in allied health appears to be a simple matter because instruction is competency based, and thus there is a common format at each instructional level. However, in this as in other academic programs, articulation is often elusive because of strong overt and covert resistance to change. Professional elitism and resistance to change are the strongest barriers.

Professional Elitism. Professional elitism is perhaps the most formidable barrier. When faculty believe in and are committed to providing students with career mobility, the negotiation of transfer agreements is relatively easy. However, when they believe that their own level of preparation is superior—one might call it professional ethnocentrism—articulation will be difficult and at times impossible.

Faculty will tend to give what at first glance appear to be good reasons for failing to develop agreements. For example, they will maintain that accreditation standards will not permit it. However, we often found that, far from preventing articulation, allied health accreditation standards often encouraged it when the emphasis was on preparing qualified entry-level practitioners within the framework of competency-based education.

Resistance to Change. Generally speaking, there are four levels of individual readiness: The first group consists of those who openly resist the prospect of articulation relationships in destructive ways. The second group consists of those who resist covertly. Those in the third group are unsure but willing to listen, and those in the fourth are very positive and take an active part in the change process. We have found that it is best to begin with the few who are interested. These early adopters can help to build an important coalition of support.

The psychology of group dynamics suggests some ways for working with the resistant. First, involve potential resisters in fact gathering. Let them help to gather information about such questions as the percentage of students within the class who are transfer students, projections of future enrollment, or projections of the number of eighteen- to twenty-one-year-olds. Having to seek out such data can have a greater impact on people's perceptions of articulation than information presented to them by someone else.

Second, help those who will be affected to make their feelings known. One effective technique is to have a committee rule that there can be no silence in the case of disagreement. The basis for the difference of opinion must be shared with the group.

Third, provide a supportive climate for dealing with the "undiscussable." One fear that emerged during our project was that students would be stolen from the hospital-based and community college programs. To deal with this anxiety, the discipline advisory groups made it clear that all transfer agreements would stipulate that students had completed the graduation requirements of the sending institution.

Fourth, communicate, confront, share, and probe. Obviously, it is much easier to remain silent, but people support what they build and need to build together.

Fifth, be patient. At times, you may want to pick up your course outlines and go home. Patience will help you through the arduous process of comparing curricula, especially with faculty who have a penchant for wanting to explain each nuance of an objective.

Sixth, plan intercollege visits. Such visits give everyone a personal view of the resources in each program and help to build mutual respect and trust among group members.

Seventh, do not allow those who oppose the change to gain ownership of academic standards. The opponents to development of transfer agreements will often try to argue that accepting your credits will have the effect of lowering the academic standards and integrity of their own programs. For this reason, proponents of articulation who emphasize sound curriculum development and standards will deprive their opponents of a very powerful weapon. Symbols and images are important, and change agents must capture the symbol and images valued by other constituencies.

Eighth, accept that this is a very passion-filled process—conflict is natural. Remember that what you are dealing with is very dear to the hearts of faculty: what they teach, how they teach it, when they teach it, and so forth. Yet, working through conflict about territorial rights and vested interests successfully provides a basis for mutual respect and reduces the fear of future conflict.

Last, realize that the formality of change may remain only a formality in the absence of follow-up. One group shared a small lament with the task force: No one had ever transferred under its transfer agreement, because no one had passed the examinations to take the upper-level courses. A closer look revealed that senior faculty were giving exams that covered advanced instead of introductory course material. An effective evaluation system is needed to determine whether anything has really changed as a result of your agreements.

Postscript

Undoubtedly, one of the reasons why the process of articulation presented here has been successful is that it was housed in a state coordinating body. However, this fact was only one of many variables. Currently, the College of Health and Human Services at Eastern Michigan University is working to develop transfer agreements with eight community colleges. We have adapted parts of the model from Kentucky. The problems are basically the same, yet so are the rewards.

References

Kentucky Council on Higher Education. *Kentucky and Health Sciences Education. Part 2. Allied Health: Comprehensive Planning for Higher Education.* Frankfort: Kentucky Council on Higher Education, 1975.

Kirchner, J. M. *State System of Allied Health Education.* Washington, D.C.: U.S. Department of Health and Human Services, 1978.

May, B. J. "Competency-Based Education: General Concepts." *Journal of Allied Health,* 1979, *8* (3), 166–171.

Elizabeth C. King is dean of the College of Health and Human Services at Eastern Michigan University. As associate director for allied health education at the Council on Higher Education, Kentucky, she was project director of the Kentucky Allied Health Project.

Where public articulation mandates are few, community colleges must devise their own approaches to articulation. The Dallas County Community College District has updated the traditional student services approach to transfer advisement with an extensive hard copy information system.

An Information-Driven Articulation Model

Richard D. McCrary

Where senior colleges are perceived to be in the driver's seat in a state or system that has no mandated articulation agreements, community colleges may see themselves as playing the role of supplicant, and senior institutions describe the issue of articulation as a community college issue. Under such conditions, the need for the accurate and timely information that helps to effectuate transfer is seen as a community college problem. The establishment of effective communication with senior institutions can help to change the perception that articulation is a problem belonging solely to community colleges.

Texas is typical of states where the community colleges have been left to their own devices in engaging the senior colleges in discussions about articulation and in soliciting basic transfer information. The Coordinating Board for State Colleges and Universities has established certain rules and regulations regarding the transfer of credit from one publicly supported institution to another. There is a core curriculum, although the total number of courses and credit hours is small and hardly accounts for the sixty or so semester hours of the freshman-sophomore years.

Much time and collaborative effort have been spent in coordinating board projects by both two- and four-year faculty and administrators to outline the courses that students should take during the first two years

C. Prager (ed.). *Enhancing Articulation and Transfer.*
New Directions for Community Colleges, no. 61. San Francisco: Jossey-Bass, Spring 1988.

of study in specific majors. However, these recommendations do not apply to the private colleges. Moreover, once such projects have been completed and adopted by the coordinating board, public institutions may ignore them. In such a context, it is necessary for the community colleges to develop effective articulation relationships with a large number of institutions, both public and private. It is also necessary to develop an effective information system that will provide students with timely and accurate data about transfer requirements and conditions at other institutions.

The Dallas County Community College District Articulation Program: A Student-Centered Approach

The Dallas County Community College District is composed of seven community colleges enrolling approximately 47,000 credit students, about half in designated transfer programs. Academic advisement is one of the primary responsibilities of the seven counseling centers. While faculty may be involved in the process, the bulk of the advisement load falls on approximately sixty-five professional counselors and a number of paraprofessionals. Because of the large number of people involved in the advisement process and the lack of statewide articulation mandates, knowledge about the transferability of courses takes on added importance. The district has developed a three-component process to meet the resulting need. This process makes use of an articulation expert, faculty discipline curriculum committees, and print information.

Articulation Expert. For the last several years, the district has housed articulation efforts in a single office, which in effect acts as the clearinghouse for transfer information. The articulation expert works out of the district office of student and international programs with liaisons from the seven community college counseling centers to identify the senior colleges with which to articulate and the types of materials needed in order to advise students about transfer. By working with the liaisons, who in turn work with counselors, faculty advisers, paraprofessionals, and students, the expert can ensure that the information is collected and disseminated in a timely and useful fashion. It is the overall responsibility of the expert to establish effective working relationships with personnel at four-year institutions, to be knowledgeable about both the district and the senior college curricula, and to develop effective dissemination processes and materials for the seven community colleges.

Faculty Discipline Curriculum Committees. The expert must also maintain a working relationship with the district's thirty-five faculty discipline curriculum committees. The committees are charged with responsibility for reviewing courses within the various disciplines and for making appropriate revisions based on curriculum decisions at the senior institutions that have transfer implications for the community colleges.

Print Information. Those who actually advise students about transfer have extensive resources of hard copy information at their disposal. These resources include course-by-course equivalency guides, brief transfer guides, course selection guides, discipline course transfer sheets, and the transfer admission guide.

The course-by-course equivalency guide is an annual compilation based on responses from twenty-two colleges and universities in Texas. The guide indicates the transferability of district courses for each receiving institution in terms of equivalency to a specific senior level course, nonequivalency but acceptability for transfer credit, or nonacceptability for credit.

The brief transfer guides are made available to academic divisions so that faculty advisers and members of curriculum committees can identify how their courses transfer.

The discipline course transfer sheets, which are disseminated to academic divisions and curriculum committees, indicate how the courses within a given academic division transfer to the ten institutions to which district students transfer most frequently. This information is useful for curriculum review as well as for transfer advisement.

Although they are often the most difficult to consolidate, the course selection guides are probably the most useful print advisement tool. By using the course-by-course equivalency guides and college catalogues, the articulation expert develops tables indicating every community college course required in a specific major for transfer to selected colleges and universities. Before dissemination to college counseling centers, the guides are verified by the senior institutions. Up to thirty-five majors have already been analyzed in this way.

The transfer admission guide explains transfer admission requirements, application procedures, and general transfer of course work at fourteen Texas four-year institutions. It is produced in booklet and chart formats in order to save those involved in the transfer process the time and effort required to locate and peruse individual catalogues. Although this document is based on catalogue information, it is also sent to the four-year institutions for verification before printing.

Interinstitutional Communication

While there may be specific exceptions to this pattern in Texas, it is generally the community college that initiates the contact with senior institutions in order to develop accurate articulation information. It is obvious that the process depends on the readiness of the senior institutions to respond to requests for transfer-related information. The role of the articulation expert in building a solid relationship with his or her contact at the university—usually the registrar—is therefore critical. Colleges that are slow to respond can usually be prompted to do so by reminders that their major competitors for transfer students will be included in such documents as the course selection guide and that they will be excluded unless they contribute up-to-date information.

The district's reliance on print information to help to effectuate transfer should not obscure the fact that the district pursues many other kinds of articulation contact with the upper-level institutions. For example, the district participates in college days sponsored by area universities for the community colleges. These events help to convince the senior institution that in advising the university's future students, the community college is providing a service to the university as well as to its own students.

The Dallas County Community College District also participates in a variety of state and regional articulation councils or bodies involving two- and four-year colleges. Membership on these councils tends to be from within the student services and administrative units of the colleges, rather than from the academic. For example, the North Texas Articulation Council is composed of representatives, most from the admissions offices, of fifteen institutions of higher education who meet to maintain an ongoing dialogue about articulation information and problems encountered in the transfer process.

Individual faculty and their contact with the four-year institutions from which many have graduated provide other valuable contacts for the resolution of articulation difficulties.

Future of Articulation

In one North Texas Articulation Council project, three institutions send transcripts to one another electronically. This project offers great promise. As institutions join the network, the cost per transcript should drop. It is expected that all colleges and universities in Texas may participate in the electronic transcript system within the next five to seven years. At that point, it should become much easier to generate information about course transfer, since transcripts could easily carry the course numbers of the sending and the receiving institutions. These numbers could be fed into a computer data base that could be used to create community college student curriculum outlines with both the district's and the transfer institution's course numbers.

Richard D. McCrary is district director of student and international programs in the Dallas County Community College District, Texas.

Transfer options for occupational-technical students have not kept pace with the reality that their transfer rates approximate those of liberal arts and science students in community college programs.

The Other Transfer Degree

Carolyn Prager

> *"How am I to get in?" asked Alice again, in a louder tone.*
> *"Are you to get in at all?" said the Footman. "That's the first question, you know."*
> *It was, no doubt: only Alice did not like to be told so. "It's really dreadful," she muttered to herself, "the way all the creatures argue. It's enough to drive one crazy!"*
> *Carroll*
> Alice in Wonderland

Alice's bemused exchange with the Fish-Footman is in many ways analogous to the experience of community college A.A.S. or related degree graduates who seek to transfer into an upper-level program. While critics have deplored the impact of growth in vocational programs on traditional transfer education, and educators have ignored the transfer needs of career students, students have resolved their predicament in much the same way as Alice does when she simply opens the door and goes in. If her subsequent experience is somewhat strange—this is the occasion when she first encounters the pig-baby and the Cheshire Cat—well, that is the way things are in Wonderland.

How many so-called nontransfer students transfer? When, where, why, and how do they transfer? Are the programs that they enter the optimal continuation of or complement to their associate degree studies? The last question is qualitative, and it cannot be answered with much

C. Prager (ed.). *Enhancing Articulation and Transfer.*
New Directions for Community Colleges, no. 61. San Francisco: Jossey-Bass, Spring 1988.

assurance if the quantitative questions are not attended to. However, it is unlikely that we will respond to the quantitative questions until we first agree that the problem of program match for career track students deserves a great deal more inquiry. There are only three general disciplinary areas in which the question of program design for occupational-technical students who transfer has been dealt with on a broad scale. The first involves certain fields of allied health where a centralizing governing authority has promoted systemwide articulation, as in Kentucky and North Carolina (Chapter Seven in this volume). The second encompasses those engineering technologies in which a national body, the Accreditation Board for Engineering and Technology, has guided articulation (Chapter Five in this volume). The third concerns business programs where many community college practitioners feel that transfer with the A.A.S. or related degree has been discouraged by another national accreditation body, the American Assembly of Collegiate Schools of Business (Chapter Six in this volume).

The Career Track Transfer Population

What do we know about the transfer of students with the A.A.S. or related degree? One sure way of answering this question is that we know less about them than we do about A.A. and A.S. degree recipients—and we know very little about them. The problem of collecting global transfer data for any category of community college student is complicated by wide intra- and intersystem and state variations in focus and methodology (Cohen, 1979). The transfer data now collected are seldom solicited for or segregated by occupational-technical degree holders. Nevertheless, there are indications that the size of this population is substantial, as high as 50 percent or more of all community college transferees since the mid 1970s (Cohen and Brawer, 1982). Unfortunately, major longitudinal studies rarely include transfer rates for community college career track students. A study at the City University of New York covering an eleven-year period (Lavin and others, 1984) shows that 45 percent of the regularly admitted community college students who entered CUNY in 1970 and 28 percent who entered under open-admissions policies completed their degrees. National data suggest that at least half of the two-year college graduates who persist and transfer over the long term obtain the baccalaureate degree (Pascarella, Smart, and Ethington, 1986). However, in the absence of better-differentiated data, these studies tell us little about the persistence and completion rates of career track students.

While the number and percentage of community college students transferring with liberal arts and science degrees have declined steadily for more than a decade, the number and percentage of those with occupational-technical degrees who transfer appears to have increased. According to Lombardi (1979), 36 percent of the two-year degree transfers within the California State University system in the late 1970s and 30 percent within the State University of New York (SUNY) system in 1974 were from career track programs. SUNY is one of the few large systems to segregate transfer data by general degree category. In the 1975-76 academic year, 5,657 associate degree students transferred into its four-year programs—3,415 with A.A./A.S. degrees and 2,242 with A.A.S./A.O.S. degrees. In the 1982-83 year, 4,445 transferred—2,145 with A.A./A.S. degrees and 2,299 with A.A.S./A.O.S. degrees. While the number of traditional transferees declined by 1,269, or 37 percent, in this period, the number of career transferees remained fairly steady. However, as a percent of total transfers, A.A.S./A.O.S. graduates increased from 39.6 percent in 1975-76 to 51.7 percent in 1982-83 (Bader-Borel, 1984).

Despite data limitations—for example, we do not know from which programs these students came or into which programs they went—the SUNY data support the claim that there are more career track-oriented transferees than there are non-career track-oriented transferees, at least for one major system in a recent period. Moreover, occupational-technical students do not start thinking about transfer late in their community college experience. Vocational students who say that they intend to transfer at the beginning of their studies—25 percent, according to Hunter and Sheldon (1980)—may be supplying more than socially acceptable answers. (Of course, the restricted data obscure the correlation between those who say they wish to transfer and those who actually do.)

Negative Context of Discussion. The framework for discussion of the career student transfer phenomenon has not been positive. Typically, it occurs in connection with perceived causal connections between increasing vocational emphases and decreasing liberal arts and science emphases that have devalued the traditional community college transfer function (Kissler, 1982; Bernstein, 1986; Richardson and Bender, 1985; Karabel, 1986). However, Cohen and Brawer (1982) maintain that the pursuit of career curricula may have greater intrinsic value than such perspectives allow, precisely because it may cultivate concern about career mobility. This in turn may stimulate student aspirations beyond the associate degree.

The climate of negativity that surrounds most discussion of community college vocationalism and its effects on the transfer phenomenon has its semantic correlative in the terminology used to describe curricula. Although the term is clearly obsolete in terms of transfer evidence, one can still find intentional usage of *terminal* to describe community college vocational programs (see, for example, the foreword to Richardson and Bender, 1985, which was written by a third party). Cohen and Brawer (1982) question whether *occupational* and *transfer* still serve to make meaningful distinctions. Nevertheless, what is implied by such terms as *colle-*

giate, university/college parallel, transfer-oriented, or *academic-oriented,* which are now used to differentiate noncareer from so-called career programs, although both types of programs lead almost equally today to baccalaureate degree studies?

Articulation Formats for Career Track Transfer

Limited Literature Discussion. Given the size and complexity of the career track transfer population, surprisingly little has been written about articulation formats that address their needs and problems. The literature does not focus on ways in which two-year and four-year institutions can best accommodate the academic aspirations and intellectual growth of the occupational-technical student before and after transfer. This is not quite the same thing as saying that there is no activity related to career program articulation. There is, but it does not take place within the context of larger discussion among those in the profession. With the exception of the debate now raging over the AACSB position on business program transfer, the literature of articulation speaks seldom if ever to the larger academic question of what constitutes the best kind of education at the baccalaureate level for students who come from the community college without the liberal arts and science credential.

Limited Transfer Options. Almost two decades ago, Walsh (1970) noted that there were few education options for vocational-technical program completers outside of a bachelor's degree in occupational education or in technology. He described a situation where the "two-year occupational graduate may be ready to articulate but has no place to go" (p. 51). Except for the interest shown primarily by allied health and engineering technology academic leaders in 2+2 programs that retain students within a specialized area of study, there is little evidence that change has been commensurate with student needs and interests. In the meantime, career program graduates have found someplace to go, conceivably not all the 2+2 programs, although we do not know where.

Advantages of Structured over Mechanical Models. Much of the current articulation activity focuses on the compilation of course equivalency guides and negotiation of program-to-program transfer agreements by individual institutions. These approaches often result in loss of credit toward the four-year degree. The same is true of unstructured transfer from occupational-technical curricula that are not protected by a formal articulation design.

Once agreed to, structured designs help to depoliticize the articulation process for students, faculty, and institutions. From the perspective of program continuity and credit integrity on transfer, these designs may be more effective for articulation of career programs than negotiation of special agreements or course equivalency lists. A recent study of 4,300 student records from a midwestern university that accepted students from seven community colleges over an eight-year period found that 2+2 students required even fewer hours for the bachelor's degree than students who had completed traditional transfer programs or who were covered by special interinstitutional agreements (Swift, 1986).

Contract Major, Capstone, and 2+2 Models. Apart from special agreements, there are three general formats for career program articulation: the contract major, the capstone, and the 2+2 program. The first two formats are little described in the literature. The contract major was developed in the 1970s at the School of Technical Careers (STC) at Southern Illinois University-Carbondale. It utilized the total resources of the university to format an individual program of study for the occupational-technical degree transfer student. This approach transfers the associate degree in full as the major, in effect reversing the sequence of traditional baccalaureate study (Walsh, 1970). The capstone program at Wayne State University accepts the technical degree in full and leads to a Bachelor in General Studies. It is specifically designed to respond to concerns about the gap between vocational and liberal arts studies (Rollyson, 1986), something that 2+2 programs do not do. In the 2+2 model, students move from a two-year degree to a four-year degree in a specialized field, without repeating previous course work and according to a more or less fixed curriculum sequence. In some cases, such as at the New Jersey Institute of Technology (Chapter Five in this volume), the senior institution restricts itself to offering only the last two years of study in certain curricula.

Cohen and Brawer (1982, p. 219) observe that "the major change in the latter half of the 1970s most often overlooked by observers was that career programs in community colleges increasingly became feeders to senior institutions, which were undergoing their own form of vocationalization." The feeding and vocationalization of four-year colleges have not been viewed uniformly by the latter as compatible and complementary activities. However, when the four-year colleges have done so, the results have been positive. Arizona State University receives 40 percent of its junior class from Maricopa Community College by restricting the size of its freshman class and by articulating upper-division programs in several areas, including career programs. Wayne State University, a Carnegie 1 research institution, offers its capstone program to assert its urban mission and to maintain the enrollment viability of its weekend college (Rollyson, 1986). The New Jersey Institute of Technology recognizes that the community colleges fulfill a valuable and costly function in preparing students for the junior year, which the Institute would otherwise have to do. Community college transfers in 1986 made up 50 percent of its graduating class. Enlightened self-interest may yet prove to be the most effective corrective to the widely perceived breakdown in articulation between the major sectors of higher education.

Policy Barriers to Articulation

The vocationalization of American higher education over the past decade or so has occurred in a period of declining resources. One might expect cost imperatives to have played a larger role in requiring the coordination of fiscal resources, facilities, faculty, and enrollments in two- and four-year colleges offering related career-oriented programs—that is, in defining articulation as something more than the mechanical movement of students from one curriculum to another. However, the social and public mandate to do so has not been present in sufficient force, creating the resultant lag between vocational program development and vocational program articulation within higher education.

Institutionalization of the High School–Community College Connection. In their desire to define a unique mission for the community college within higher education, community college leaders at the national level have in the past decade advocated the strengthening of secondary-postsecondary partnerships involving vocational education. This attractive agenda has an immediate appeal to taxpayers who must pay the freight for both public school and community college education at the local level. Nonetheless, it has diverted attention from the more traditional linkages between two-year colleges and other sectors of higher education by placing the emphasis on the secondary-postsecondary continuum rather than on the secondary-higher education continuum.

In 1978, the American Association of Community and Junior Colleges and the American Vocational Association jointly sponsored a project that set out to analyze what fosters and what impedes interinstitutional cooperation (Bushnell, 1978). Five case studies typify exemplary practices at the local level. Each involves a community college and an area vocational school. Only one describes articulation beyond the associate degree, and that is for one program only. Thus, that occupational-technical program articulation has been institutionalized as a secondary-postsecondary phenomenon occurs well before Parnell's (1985) attention to the "neglected majority," which advances terminal vocational education for the majority of the population who will never obtain a baccalaureate degree. The dovetailing of specialized technical education for the "neglected majority" does not extend upward to a four-year diploma on the grounds that 83 percent of the population does not have the baccalaureate, and only two of the twenty fastest-growing occupations require it. This espousal of a declining social mission for the community colleges at once disparages aspiration beyond the associate degree and sanctions a downward direction to career program articulation.

Federal Funding. Since *Adams* v. *Califano,* the federal Vocational Education Act has sought to allocate federal funds and drive state funds for program improvement and development on the basis of socioeconomic and demographic criteria that target funds to the economically and educationally disadvantaged. The net effect is that the bulk of the allocation in many states goes to urban areas with high minority concentrations. However, the act restricts funding specifically to subbaccalaureate activity. This means that counseling services that would assist career students in transferring or curriculum articulation efforts between a community and a senior college (but not between a community college and an area vocational and technical school) are precluded from fiscal support. Thus, a potentially powerful agent mandating the improvement of occupational-technical educational opportunity for the disadvantaged has built-in provisos that limit the academic attainment of those whom it is designed to serve.

Calls for Transfer Renewal

The assertion that community colleges de facto depress academic expectations, educational persistence, and economic potential has dominated criticisms of the community colleges for almost three decades (Karabel, 1986; Pincus, 1986). A major component of the assertion is the claim that community colleges shunt students into vocational programs.

The criticism has given rise to calls for renewal of mission by reaffirming the primacy of the transfer function and by developing strong working relationships with other colleges and universities (Deegan, Tillery, and Melone, 1985; Cross, 1985; Bernstein, 1986). Career student transfer is not expressly included in these calls, except for the problematic dimension that it has given to the perceived crisis in transfer. In these and parallel discussions, programmatic application of the transfer function is understood to mean transfer from liberal arts and science curricula, although there is much evidence of transfer interest and activity on the part of career track students.

Response to the Ford Foundation's Urban Community College Transfer Opportunities Program moves the definition of transfer function from the theoretical to the actual. Granted, many of the first-phase project designs at funded colleges encompassed comprehensive transfer services—student information systems, counseling, mentoring, and so forth—that could be directed equally to career track and to non-career track students. While several projects also contained program-to-program articulation activities, only two of the twenty-four community colleges initially supported by Ford had significant components dedicated specifically to the promotion of transfer from career programs. Cuyahoga Community College sought to address weak student preparation by developing an articulation model for three vocational-technical curricula with area secondary schools and four-year colleges, and La Guardia Community College, with 85 percent of its enrollments in career programs, sought to enhance the transfer function by developing a design for A.A.S. degree program transfer through articulation of its accounting curriculum to that of Baruch College, an institution noted for its strong business curricula.

At issue ultimately is the question of whether the A.A.S. and related degrees represent a valid route to the baccalaureate, one that cultivates educational and presumably social and career mobility. That the value of career-oriented education should not be decided on such narrow grounds as "simplistic data on job entry and first salary" (Cohen and Brawer, 1982, p. 24) is a point well made. Certainly, the evidence does not support the notion that the pursuit of an A.A.S. degree in and of itself curtails desire for or pursuit of still higher degrees by comparison to the transfer aspirations and actual transfer of those who pursue other associate degrees. In a survey of recent graduates from La Guardia, just under half expressed interest in furthering their education in the near future for job-related reasons; only 8 percent expressed no interest in continuing their education (Kane, Parsons, and Associates, Inc., 1984).

Even if it were true that over the long term the earning power of the A.A.S. degree is less than the earning power of any bachelor's degree, it cannot be denied that the earning power of those who enter the job market with only the A.A.S. degree is on the whole greater than that of those with any other combination of two years of undergraduate work. For most people, career mobility means the desire to increase economic options. The possibility of doing so over the short term has understandable appeal to those who have not had such options. The access role of community college career programs as a motive force—for initial entry into higher education and for continuing on by those who might otherwise not do so—should be an important focus of future research.

Toward an Agenda

A great deal of critical energy continues to be expended bemoaning the vocationalization of the community college. These laments often take place in a context deploring the weakening of an earlier primary sector mission to provide transfer education parallel to the education provided by the first two years of traditional university arts and science education; but that was then, and this is now. This is not to say that we should abandon attempts to revive and strengthen liberal education at the community college and thereby encourage more extensive transfer with arts and science degrees. However misguided it may be, students' concern about career outcomes shows no sign of abating at any level of higher education. If current trends persist, the career degree recipient will continue to seek a bachelor's degree, with or without our informed assistance and direction. If we accept that the transfer of occupational-technical graduates is a healthy and viable phenomenon, it then behooves us to demonstrate at least as much concern about these students' transfer options and education as we do about the more traditional transfer degrees. How can this be done?

Improving the Data Base. One way of demonstrating such concern is by paying considerably greater attention to the collection and coordination of transfer data, minimally by degree category and maximally by major, race, sex, employment status, and funding source of baccalaureate education, such as tuition reimbursement by employers. Inquiry is also needed into how effectively occupational-technical curricula prepare students for transfer.

Improving General Education. Quantitative limitations on general education courses in career program sequences should not fix the qualitative limit. There are at least three ways of maximizing general education. The first is through review of overall distribution requirements to see whether more credits should be allocated to liberal studies. The pressure from program participants to add or substitute yet another career-specific course should be resisted. The second is through analysis of credits already allocated to see whether they are in courses as substantively rigorous as those in the arts and science programs—in other words, to question seriously such quasi-collegiate courses as "Math for the Health Sciences" and "Business Writing." The third and most important is to teach career-specific courses with increased attention to the building of conceptual and communication skills. This is especially important in competency-based areas where competency tends to be measured by short, so-called objective responses.

Improving Preparatory Programs. Admission to the more rigorous occupational-technical programs tends to be based on demonstrated competence in mathematics and science. Amelioration of deficiencies in these areas usually requires a bridge between elementary basic skills and college-level work. One approach is through compensatory "tech-prep" courses that combine mathematics, laboratory science, and hands-on exposure to career areas.

Improving Transfer. Finally, we need to widen career students' opportunities for transfer in several ways. Where umbrella articulation policies exist, they should be examined for parity. For example, do the same general education courses receive equal transfer credit when they are taken by A.A./A.S. and A.A.S. or related degree students? Next, community college leaders need to encourage program articulation with and by senior institutions. This can be accomplished in part by increasing the pressure on program approval and review bodies (whether state, system, or college) to ensure curriculum development and implementation on the 2+2 model. At the same time, community colleges should examine the transfer potential of each career program and seek transfer options for it. They should also seek delivery modes that are compatible with the needs of time- and location-bound community college students who wish to obtain a bachelor's degree. For example, the senior college can be invited to offer instruction on the community college campus through evening and weekend programs.

The community college should consider education about transfer to be an important facet of occupational-technical education and take steps to ensure that each degree aspirant and recipient becomes aware of the advantages of, opportunities for, and prerequisites for continuing. Community colleges have a vested interest in demonstrating that they prepare people for further education. As an extension of transfer education, they should guide and monitor each career student's application through the wonderland of transfer, intervening for the student if necessary to forestall potential arbitrary credit loss or inappropriate design in the four-year program. Certainly, the community college is in a better position than the student to negotiate individual transfer disputes. Given the frequent lag between graduation and transfer, the community college should continue to provide such services for graduates well after graduation, perhaps levying a fee to offset costs, much as other colleges and universities continue to provide ongoing career placement services for their graduates.

References

Bader-Borel, P. (ed.). *Compilation of Statistical Data Concerning the Community Colleges of the State University of New York, 1983–1984.* Albany: Office for Community Colleges, Office of Finance and Business, and Office of Institutional Research and Planning, State University of New York, 1984. 368 pp. (ED 253 280)

Bernstein, A. "The Devaluation of Transfer: Current Explanations and Possible Causes." In L. S. Zwerling (ed.), *The Community College and Its Critics.* New Directions for Community Colleges, no. 54. San Francisco: Jossey-Bass, 1986.

Bushnell, D. S. *Education and Training: A Guide to Interinstitutional Cooperation. Final Report.* Washington, D.C.: American Association of Community and Junior Colleges, 1978. 341 pp. (ED 174 831)

Cohen, A. M. *Counting the Transfer Students: ERIC Junior College Resource Review.* Los Angeles: ERIC Clearinghouse for Junior Colleges, 1979. 6 pp. (ED 172 864)

Cohen, A. M., and Brawer, F. B. *The American Community College.* San Francisco: Jossey-Bass, 1982.

Cross, K. P. "Determining Missions and Priorities for the Fifth Generation." In W. L. Deegan, D. Tillery, and Associates, *Renewing the American Community College: Priorities and Strategies for Effective Leadership.* San Francisco: Jossey-Bass, 1985.

Deegan, W. L., Tillery, D., and Melone, R. J. "The Process of Renewal: An Agenda for Action." In W. L. Deegan, D. Tillery, and Associates, *Renewing the American Community College: Priorities and Strategies for Effective Leadership.* San Francisco, Jossey-Bass, 1985.

Hunter, R., and Sheldon, M. S. *Statewide Longitudinal Study: Report on Academic*

Year 1979-80. Part III. Fall 1979—Results. Woodland Hills, Calif.: Los Angeles Pierce College, 1980. 95 pp. (ED 188 714)

Kane, Parsons, and Associates, Inc. *Attitudes of Recent La Guardia Graduates Towards Further Education: A Baseline Measurement. Report of Findings.* New York: La Guardia Community College, 1984. 49 pp. (ED 271 148)

Karabel, J. "Community Colleges and Social Stratification in the 1980s." In L. S. Zwerling (ed.), *The Community College and Its Critics.* New Directions for Community Colleges, no. 54. San Francisco: Jossey-Bass, 1986.

Kissler, G. R. "The Decline of the Transfer Function: Threats or Challenges?" In F. C. Kintzer (ed.), *Improving Articulation and Transfer Relationships.* New Directions for Community Colleges, no. 39. San Francisco: Jossey-Bass, 1982.

Lavin, D. E., and others. *Long-Term Graduation Rates of Students at the City University of New York.* New York: Office of Institutional Research and Analysis, City University of New York, 1984. 28 pp. (ED 247 858)

Lombardi, J. A. *The Decline of Transfer Education.* Topical Paper no. 70. Los Angeles: ERIC Clearinghouse for Junior Colleges, 1979. 37 pp. (ED 179 273)

Parnell, D. *The Neglected Majority.* Washington, D.C.: Community College Press, 1985. 189 pp. (ED 262 843)

Pascarella, E. T., Smart, J. C., and Ethington, C. A. "Long-Term Persistence of Two-Year College Students." Paper presented at the annual meeting of the Association for the Study of Higher Education, San Antonio, Tex., Feb. 20-23, 1986. 48 pp. (ED 268 900)

Pincus, F. L. "Vocational Education: More False Promises." In L. S. Zwerling (ed.), *The Community College and Its Critics.* New Directions for Community Colleges, no. 54. San Francisco: Jossey-Bass, 1986.

Richardson, R. C., Jr., and Bender, L. W. *Students in Urban Settings: Achieving the Baccalaureate Degree.* ASHE-ERIC Higher Education Report no. 6. Washington, D.C.: Association for the Study of Higher Education, 1985. 90 pp. (ED 265 798)

Rollyson, C. E., Jr. "Capstone: The Community College-University Connection." *Community College Review,* 1986, *14* (1), 40-45.

Swift, J. S., Jr. "The Community College Transfer and 'Plus Two' Programs: Access to a Baccalaureate Degree in Four Years?" *Community/Junior College Quarterly of Research and Practice,* 1986, *10* (4), 307-316.

Walsh, M. E. "Articulation Problems of Vocational-Technical Students." *Community College Review,* 1970, *3,* 50-54.

Carolyn Prager is former vice-president for academic affairs at Hudson County Community College and former state director of community colleges for New Jersey.

This chapter provides an annotated bibliography of ERIC documents and journal articles on national, state, and institutional efforts to improve articulation.

Sources and Information: Policy and Practice in Articulation and Transfer

Anita Y. Colby, Mary P. Hardy

From the beginning of the two-year college movement, agreements have existed between two- and four-year colleges concerning the transfer of students. Over the years, informal arrangements have been replaced with formal, documented agreements by and between single institutions that cover course equivalencies and program and curriculum articulation.

In the past fifteen years, broad efforts have been made at the state, regional, and institutional levels to facilitate the smooth flow of students from high schools to community colleges to baccalaureate-granting institutions. These efforts have extended beyond the articulation and transfer of course credits. Community colleges have become involved in programs to improve the academic skills of high school students before they enter postsecondary education; in agreements that use student competencies as the basis of course and program articulation; in activities aimed at identifying, assessing, and tracking potential transfer students early in their postsecondary careers; and in the development of information systems to monitor and promote students' academic progress.

This chapter is an annotated bibliography of recent ERIC documents dealing with articulation. The documents and journal articles

C. Prager (ed.). *Enhancing Articulation and Transfer.*
New Directions for Community Colleges, no. 61. San Francisco: Jossey-Bass, Spring 1988.

described in this chapter were selected from materials added to the ERIC data base since 1980. The chapter is divided into five sections: national, state, and regional efforts to improve articulation; statewide vocational education articulation; articulation of the liberal arts curriculum; articulation of the vocational curriculum; and articulated health occupations programs.

National, State, and Regional Efforts to Improve Articulation

Avila, J. G., Baller, M. J., Brown, S. E., Vera, R. T., Blackwell, A. G., and Menocal, A. M. *Petition to Increase Minority Transfer from Community Colleges to State Four-Year Schools.* San Francisco: Mexican American Legal Defense and Educational Fund, Inc., and Public Advocacy, Inc., 1983. 37 pp. (ED 237 134)

This document examines the current status of transfers of minority students from two-year colleges to state four-year institutions. Statistics about the concentration of minority students in two-year colleges and their low transfer rates indicate that California's three sectors of higher education—the California community colleges, the California State University system, and the University of California—have violated state law. The authors suggest ways of improving the transfer function by focusing on the provision of adequate counseling and transfer information for students, improving articulation, increasing the uniformity of course numbering and content, and improving preparation and services.

California Community Colleges, Office of the Chancellor. *Identifying and Assisting Transfer Students: Survey of Current Policies and Practices.* Sacramento: Office of the Chancellor, California Community Colleges, 1982. 42 pp. (ED 223 277)

This study sought to determine the policies and practices of the state's 106 community colleges regarding potential transfer students. Community colleges were asked to provide information about social programs and activities aimed at identifying and assisting potential transfer students, the success of these activities, the role of faculty in facilitating transfer, required individual or group advisement, and articulation efforts with other educational levels and to make recommendations for improvements in current practices. Thirty-four percent of the colleges responding felt that a more formal matriculation procedure would improve the identification of potential transfers. Sixty-nine percent of the schools had formal articulation agreements with four-year institutions, and 52 percent had regular liaisons with local high schools. The survey instrument is included.

California State Postsecondary Education Commission. *Views from the Field on Community College Transfer: Testimony to the Ad Hoc Committee on Community College Transfer of the California Postsecondary Education Commission.* Sacramento: California State Postsecondary Education Commission, 1984. 184 pp. (ED 244 669)

This report contains the testimony of individuals representing a variety of sectors of higher education in California. Prefatory material provides information on the committee's hearings and summarizes the themes that emerged. Testimony from chief executive officers, program and college administrators, representatives of faculty groups, an attorney from the Mexican American Legal Defense and Education Fund, and representatives of the Association of Independent California Colleges and Universities and each segment of public postsecondary education in California suggests that articulation needs to begin with the lower grades and continue through the graduate level and that transfer problems cannot be solved by any one segment of education or by any group of people acting alone.

Florida State Department of Education. *Interpretations of the Articulation Agreement.* Tallahassee: Florida State Department of Education, 1982. 82 pp. (ED 256 390)

This document contains the text of the Articulation Agreement of 1971, which was developed by the Division of Community Colleges and the State University System of Florida to provide a basic framework within which students who complete programs under specified conditions are assured that their work will be accepted when they transfer to state universities in Florida.

Florida State Postsecondary Education Commission. *Feasibility Study of a Public/Independent Articulation Agreement: Report and Recommendations of the Postsecondary Education Planning Commission. 1987-Report 1.* Tallahassee: Florida State Postsecondary Education Commission, 1987. 46 pp. (ED 280 541)

In response to a legislative mandate, a study was conducted to determine the feasibility of developing a comprehensive articulation agreement between public and nonpublic postsecondary institutions in Florida. A survey of state higher education officers in other states revealed that no state had such a comprehensive agreement. Presidents and academic officers at thirty postsecondary institutions in Florida were surveyed by telephone to determine their preference for a statewide comprehensive agreement, local agreements, or some other arrangement for articulation. The study also involved a telephone survey of registrars and admissions and articulation coordinators at thirty-two selected postsecondary institutions in the state. Survey findings and recommendations are included.

Waggaman, J. S. "Articulation Outcomes from Use of the Products and Services of the Florida Statewide Course-Numbering System." Paper presented at the 15th annual Florida Statewide Conference on Institutional Research, Orlando, June 24-25, 1982. 14 pp. (ED 248 819)

This paper discusses the results of an evaluation of the Florida Statewide Course-Numbering System (SCNS), a system designed to enhance articulation between community colleges and the state universities of Florida. Institutional liaison officers to SCNS as well as faculty members and department chair were surveyed. SCNS products and services were found to have uses in the following areas: admissions and registration, articulation and course comparability, creation of a community of scholars, counseling and advisement, curriculum analysis, funding methods and student costs, regional analysis and course comparability, and maximization of student course transfers.

Western Interstate Commission for Higher Education. *Improving the Articulation/Transfer Process Between Two- and Four-Year Institutions.* Boulder, Colo.: Western Interstate Commission for Higher Education, 1985. 450 pp. (ED 270 141)

A collaborative project involving four states in the Western Interstate Commission for Higher Education region was conducted to develop an on line student information system enabling students and their advisers to obtain current information about course and credit transfer from two- to four-year institutions. Project activities in the four states—Arizona, California, Colorado, and New Mexico, which all have a high concentration of minority students in community colleges—targeted the improvement of articulation and the transfer process. The study report includes information on pregrant activities, timelines, costs, and project results for each state. Appendixes make up the bulk of the report. They include a final evaluation of the project, materials from a project workshop, sample articulation agreements, Arizona's handbook for articulation task forces, and materials developed for specific articulation activities.

Willson, L. F., and Anderson, C. *Articulation with Four-Year Colleges. Information Item.* Sacramento: Office of the Chancellor, California Community Colleges, 1986. 10 pp. (ED 276 468)

This document provides an update on the implementation of an action plan developed in 1985 for facilitating community college articulation with high schools and four-year colleges in California. After presenting background information, the authors summarize the 1985 plan and the progress that has been made in implementing its components. A number of activities are highlighted, including the publication of the first California handbook for articulation policies and procedures, intersegmental efforts to promote faculty communication statewide, and the participation of fifty-nine colleges in the California Articulation Number system, which was designed to help students determine the community college courses that fulfill specific course requirements at four-year institutions. An action plan for 1986-87 is presented.

Zeldman, D. "Articulation and Transfer in Florida." In F. C. Kintzer (ed.), *Improving Articulation and Transfer Relationships.* New Directions for Community Colleges, no. 39. San Francisco: Jossey-Bass, 1982.

The author highlights portions of the articulation agreement between Florida's community college system and state university system and presents examples of practical efforts used to ensure the smooth transfer of students. The role of community college relations offices, aids to articulation, and current articulation programs are considered.

Statewide Vocational Education Articulation

Davis, R., Ditzenberger, R., James, M., and Lovelace, B. E. *Inservice Training for Regional Planning/Articulation of Vocational Education: A Resource Manual.* Denton: North Texas State University, 1985. 178 pp. (ED 262 164)

This guide provides instructional materials for the implementation of a regional planning and articulation project for vocational education in Texas. The project's rationale, the regional planning model, the planning process, orientation and use of the planning committee, procedures for regional planning, development and implementation of a communication system, and the process of articulation are covered. Twenty-six related handouts are included. The handouts address such issues as assessing the need for workers in priority occupations, comparing enrollment and labor market projections, administering a community occupational survey, planning a training program, developing a communication network, implementing follow-up, and tracking data flow at local, regional, and state levels.

Hamilton, J. B., Kurth, P., and Merz, H. *Ohio Vocational Education-University Linkages.* Columbus: National Center for Research in Vocational Education, Ohio State University, 1985. 82 pp. (ED 262 270)

These authors describe a study that explored alternative delivery patterns and developed a composite model designed to strengthen the linkages between universities in the state of Ohio and the Ohio Department of Education's State Division of Vocational and Career Education (SDVE). They examine aspects of the composite model, including strategies for the delivery of preservice education to nonvocational teacher educators; the supervision of new vocational personnel; pedagogical, technological, and informational update; skills testing; curriculum development and dissemination; and research and development. Recommendations to the SDVE regarding the model's implementation are included.

Knight, M. M. "Meeting the High-Technology Challenge Through Articulation: A Discussion of Inhibitors and Enhancers of Vocational Curriculum Articulation." Paper presented at the 63rd annual national convention of the American Association of Community and Junior Colleges, New Orleans, Apr. 24–27, 1983. 9 pp. (ED 231 420)

This paper discusses the ideal and the current state of articulation between community colleges and universities and between community colleges and county-level vocational schools in Florida. The author provides examples of successful community college–university articulation agreements, including a mandate that associate in arts degree students should be classified as juniors on transfer and a common course-numbering system ensuring equal credit for courses offered by both types of institutions, and offers solutions to problems associated with articulation efforts. Two case studies are included.

Radcliffe, C. W., and Zirkin, B. G. *Vocational-Technical Education Program Articulation and Linkages in Maryland.* Catonsville: Institute for Policy Analysis and Research, University of Maryland, 1986. 80 pp. (ED 277 868)

This document describes a study that investigated the extent of cooperation between and among agencies and individuals responsible for job training, vocational-technical (voc-tech) and occupational education programs, and support services in Maryland in 1986. The survey instrument was mailed to the coordinators of voc-tech education in the twenty-four local education agencies and to deans of the seventeen community colleges, and a number of individuals connected with voc-tech education and Job Training Partnership Act Private Industry Councils were interviewed. The authors report that analyses of the data collected revealed increased interest and activity in program articulation but inadequate communication among administrators and other practitioners regarding common programs and problems. Appendixes detail current and planned activities for the coordination of voc-tech education, job training, and support services.

State Fair Community College. *A Study of Articulation in Missouri Vocational Technical Programs. Final Report.* Sedalia, Mo.: State Fair Community College, 1984. 70 pp. (ED 247 401)

This document describes a study that examined the potential for articulating students among Missouri institutions that offer vocational-technical (vo-tech) education at the secondary, postsecondary, and adult levels. The results of a survey of attitudes among administrators and instructors at four- and two-year institutions, vo-tech schools, and comprehensive high schools in the state are presented. A model for articulation is described. The model includes five strategies: Establish articulation of vocational programs as a high institutional priority, establish a joint advisory committee to facilitate coordination, obtain state support for participation in articulation, provide in-service training, and develop formal articulation agreements. Appendixes make up more than half of the report. They include the survey instrument and sample articulation materials.

Articulation of the Liberal Arts Curriculum

Baltimore Community College. *The Community College of Baltimore's Ford Foundation Bridge Project: Summary Status Report.* Baltimore, Md.: Baltimore Community College, 1984. 10 pp. (ED 273 306)

This document describes the objectives and accomplishments of the Bridge Program conducted by the Community College of Baltimore (CCB). The Bridge Program was designed to improve and extend transfer opportunities in Baltimore. It sought to develop a completely articulated arts and sciences transfer program extending from five feeder high schools to four receiving baccalaureate institutions. CCB served as the bridge between secondary education and four-year institutions. Components of the project included review, revision, and strengthening of the arts and sciences curricula at CCB; creation of formal articulation agreements based on the revised curricula; and development of a process to identify potential transfer students at the high school level.

Donovan, R. A., Schaier-Peleg, B., and Forer, B. (eds.). *Transfer: Making It Work. A Community College Report.* Washington, D.C.: American Association of Community and Junior Colleges, 1987. 75 pp. (ED 281 579)

This document provides an overview of the Ford Foundation's Urban Community College Transfer Opportunities Project, which was designed to improve the process of transfer from the community college to the four-year college for urban minority students through partnerships with secondary schools and four-year colleges and universities. Program descriptions and recommendations based on the experiences of the twenty-four colleges involved in the effort are included.

Schaier-Peleg, B. (ed.). *New Initiatives for Transfer Students. Urban Community College Transfer Opportunities Program.* Bronx, N.Y.: Networks, Bronx Community College, 1984. 69 pp. (ED 264 896)

The author examines the rationale for and the activities and outcomes of the Ford Foundation's Urban Community College Transfer

Opportunities Program. Reasons for the program's development are examined, and issues and problems related to transfer from two- to four-year colleges are discussed. The orientation, follow-up, articulation, curriculum development, student identification efforts, faculty development, honors programs, information systems, and assessment activities that were funded are described.

Stevens, R. "Restructuring the Liberal Arts: Synthesis Rather Than Fragmentation." *Liberal Education,* 1985, *71* (2), 163-165.

The author offers an alternative for liberal arts curriculum development based not on the scattershot approach taken by most core curricula but on a model of overlapping curricular circles. Each curricular circle centers on the student's major and draws together the underlying strands of a liberal education.

Young, D. F. *Enriching the Transfer Effort: The Santa Monica College Scholars Program.* Santa Monica, Calif.: Santa Monica College, 1986. 12 pp. (ED 269 069)

This report describes the development, implementation, operation, and outcomes of the Santa Monica College Scholars Program, a partnership of six colleges and universities assisting students with demonstrated academic ability to accomplish their goal of earning a baccalaureate degree. Noteworthy features of the Scholars Program include the following: guaranteed admission to any participating university, a mandatory core curriculum with restricted enrollment, discussions among faculty from each participating college regarding curriculum content and rigor, and a special support network for participating students.

Articulation of the Vocational Curriculum

Bushnell, D. S. "Articulating Vocational Education at the Postsecondary Level." In S. V. Martorana and E. Kuhns (eds.), *Transferring Experiential Credit.* New Directions for Experiential Learning, no. 4. San Francisco: Jossey-Bass, 1979.

The author views the move toward cooperative arrangements in vocational education as a response to pressures to hold down educational costs while maintaining or expanding student options. A variety of programs designed to smooth student transitions vertically from one program level to another and horizontally from one institution to another are described.

Carter, K. G. *An Articulation Model for Vocational Programs Between a Secondary Area Vocational-Technical School and a Community College in Pennsylvania.* Media, Penn.: Delaware County Community College, 1985. 163 pp. (ED 279 382)

This document reports on the development and field testing of a model for the articulation of programs between the Delaware County Area Vocational-Technical School and Delaware County Community College in Pennsylvania. Development of the model involved the following steps: formation of the Articulation Advisory Committee (AAC); preliminary meeting of faculties; first meeting of the AAC; in-service training to provide an orientation to competency-based vocational education, define the scope of the programs, and select an occupational analysis methodology; verification of the occupational analysis; incumbent worker survey; determination and validation of terminal performance objectives; development of plans for student recruitment, placement, and training and for recruitment in industry; development of criterion-referenced tests; formation of a plan for resource sharing; and formal agreement.

McNutt, A. "Developing a Technology Articulation Program: The Need for Articulation." Paper presented at the national conference of the National Council on Occupational Education, San Diego, Calif., October 15–19, 1986. 15 pp. (ED 281 582)

Nashville State Technical Institute is currently involved in an Advanced Technology Articulation Demonstration Project, a collaborative effort with Tennessee State University, two local high schools, the Tennessee Valley Authority, the Center for Occupational Research and Development, and the State Department of Education. This report describes the role of each agency in such aspects of the articulation project as curriculum development, teacher training, competency determination, project evaluation, and overall coordination. Course outlines are included.

Maricopa County Community College District. *Articulation: The Coordination of Occupational Education in Maricopa County, Arizona.* Phoenix, Ariz.: Maricopa County Community College District, 1985. 20 pp. (ED 257 513)

Key issues related to the articulation of vocational education in Maricopa County are identified and discussed. Information is provided on the district's use of contracting (the purchase of education and training that would not otherwise be available), the granting of college course credit for the mastery of competencies equivalent to a college course, acceptance of occupational credit, resource coordination, joint program development with area high schools, regionalization of public occupational education resources, and dual enrollment programs for talented high school students.

Phillips, C. G., Jr., and Kuchinsky, C. A. *A Secondary-Postsecondary Program to Prepare Master Technicians.* Richmond: Virginia State Department of Community Colleges, 1986. 46 pp. (ED 267 854)

This document describes a state-funded pilot project designed to develop a 2+2 model in electronics and electromechanical technology. Section I is an overview that includes a copy of the project agreement, lists of participating agencies, a statement of objectives, and a timetable. Section II, which focuses on curriculum development, describes research to determine entry-level competencies expected by employers; examines changes in the technical work force, phases of curriculum development, the cyclical process for forecasts of occupational demand, job opportunities in the electronics and electromechanical technology field, and new technology occupations; provides a description of the master technician (MT) program and identifies advantages of the MT approach; and illustrates student flow. Section III presents materials developed for the project's public relations effort.

Smith, A. D. "Occupational Education and College-Parallel Programs of the Two-Year College: Transfer and Credit Articulation Controversy." 32 pp. (ED 263 957)

The author reviews current developments, problems, and issues in articulation and transfer between two- and four-year colleges. The nature of the two-year college and its curriculum are discussed. Particular emphasis is placed on general education and on the effects of a commuting student body on the curriculum. College-parallel and occupational programs are contrasted in terms of their historical place in the curriculum. Major problems of transfer and articulation are discussed, and the difficulties faced by occupational students, internal problems posed by general education requirements, and the reverse transfer trend are highlighted. The document includes a series of case studies illustrating various transfer policies.

Articulated Health Occupations Programs

Gulledge, E. N. *Health Education Consortium. Articulated Nursing Education Program. Final Report from January 1, 1980, to June 30, 1981.* Niceville, Fla.: Okaloosa-Walton Junior College, 1981. 153 pp. (ED 230 686)

This document reports on a consortial effort by vocational centers, community and junior colleges, and universities in Florida's Region I district to develop an articulated nursing educational route aimed at meeting the needs of all types of nursing personnel, ranging from nurses' aides to nurses with master's in science degrees. A pilot project undertaken at Pensacola Junior College to develop an articulated licensed practical nurse and associate degree nurse program is described.

Hosch, I. *Educational Progression of Licensed Practical Nurses to Registered Nursing Programs. Project Report.* Bluefield, W. Va.: Bluefield State College, 1986. 193 pp. (ED 274 786)

This document describes a project conducted to develop a structural mechanism for articulation between Bluefield State College and Mercer County Vocational Technical Center in West Virginia to permit licensed practical nurses (LPNs) who wished to become registered nurses to transfer credits they had earned for the LPN degree and thus eliminate unnecessary repetition of some basic nursing courses. Guidelines for articulation agreements are included.

Kentucky State Council on Higher Education. *Kentucky Allied Health Project Final Report: A State System for Allied Health Education.* Frankfort: Kentucky State Council on Higher Education, 1982. 101 pp. (ED 231 300)

This report outlines the accomplishments of the Kentucky Allied Health Project, which implemented an articulation model for allied health education that sought to promote transition from one educational level to another and to foster cooperation in educational planning and resource utilization. Four models of transfer of credit and career mobility for the preprofessional, basic professional, certificate-granting basic professional, and intermediate professional curricula are described.

Anita Y. Colby is associate director of the ERIC Clearinghouse for Junior Colleges.

Mary P. Hardy is user services specialist at the ERIC Clearinghouse for Junior Colleges.

Index

C

D

E

F

G

H

I

J

K

L

M